CHECK YOUR VOCABULARY FOR LAW

a workbook for users

second edition

Original material by
David Riley

Edited and revised by
Liz Greasby

PETER COLLIN PUBLISHING

First published in Great Britain 1996
Second edition published 1998

Published by Peter Collin Publishing Ltd
1 Cambridge Road, Teddington, Middx, UK

British Library Cataloguing in Publication Data

A catalogue record for this book is available from the British Library

ISBN 1-901659-21-6

Text typeset by PCP Ltd
Printed by Latimer Trend, UK

Peter Collin Publishing
1 Cambridge Road, Teddington, TW11 8DT, UK
tel: +44 181 943 3386 fax: +44 181 943 1673
email: info@pcp.co.uk web site: www.pcp.co.uk

Introduction

The worksheets in this workbook contain a variety of exercises appropriate for students requiring a working knowledge of English law terminology. The worksheets can be used either for self-study or in the classroom and can be completed in any order. Several have 'extensions': short classroom exercises based on the language in the main exercise. All the questions within this workbook are based on the Peter Collin Publishing ***Dictionary of Law*** (ISBN 0-948549-33-5).

This workbook is aimed at students with at least an intermediate level of English. However, many people who work in the legal field have to read in English on a regular basis; students with a more basic level of English may therefore already have the passive vocabulary to handle many of the exercises.

Specialist vocabulary

It is important to appreciate that 'knowing' specialist vocabulary involves more than simply recognising it.

- You can understand the meaning of a word when reading or listening and yet be unable to remember that same word when speaking or writing.
- You may remember the word, but use it incorrectly. This can be a grammatical problem, like knowing that 'import' can be used both as a noun and as a verb. Or it may be a question of collocation: we pay *income* tax, not *revenue* tax.
- Then there is the question of the sound of the word. Can you pronounce it? And do you recognise it when you hear it pronounced?

For these reasons - memory, use and sound - it is important that students practise specialist vocabulary so that they can learn to use it more confidently and effectively. The exercises in this workbook will help students to expand their knowledge and use of legal vocabulary.

Photocopiable material

All the worksheets can be legally photocopied to use in class. If, as a teacher, you intend to use most of the book with a class you may find it more convenient for the students to buy a copy each. You are not allowed to photocopy or reproduce the front or back cover.

Using the *Dictionary of Law*

All of the vocabulary taught or practised in this workbook is in the Peter Collin Publishing *Dictionary of Law*. The ***Dictionary of Law*** gives definitions in simple English which students can read and understand. Many of the examples and definitions in the workbook are taken directly from the dictionary. Students should have a copy of the ***Dictionary of Law*** for referring to when completing the exercises; using the dictionary is an essential part of successful language learning.

Structure of a *Dictionary of Law* entry

Each entry within the dictionary includes key elements that help a student understand the definition of the term and how to use it in context. Each term has a clear example, and part of speech. This is followed by example sentences and quotations from newspapers and magazines that show how the term is used in real life. These elements of the dictionary are used to create the questions within this workbook.

Vocabulary Record Sheet

At the back of the book is a Vocabulary Record Sheet. Recording useful vocabulary in a methodical way plays a key role in language learning and could be done, for example, at the end of each lesson. The ***Dictionary of Law*** is a useful tool for ensuring that the personal vocabulary record is accurate and is a good source for example sentences to show how words are used, as well as for notes about meaning and pronunciation, etc.

Workbook Contents

Using the workbook

Most students find it easier to assimilate new vocabulary if the words are learned in related groups, rather than in isolation. For example, words frequently occur in the same context as their opposites and, as such, it makes sense to learn the pairs of opposites together (*see worksheets on pages 7 and 32*). Similarly, mind maps encourage students to look for connections between words (*see worksheet on page 9*). The exercises and activities in this workbook have all been grouped into sections. These sections practise different elements of law vocabulary, enabling the student to gain a fuller understanding of the words learnt.

The first section, **Word-building** (*pages 1-9*), encourages the student to identify links between words and to learn words that are morphologically related (for example, verbs and nouns which have the same stems). Within the **Parts of Speech** (*pages 10-23*) section, the emphasis is on understanding meanings and how to use terms in their correct grammatical forms. The worksheets in the third section practise the **Pronunciation** of legal vocabulary (*pages 24-27*). The section **Vocabulary in Context** (*pages 28-36*) includes topic-specific exercises such as categorising crimes and reconstructing the story of a case. The activities in the last section, **Puzzles & Quizzes** (*pages 37-51*), expand students' knowledge and use of vocabulary in a fun way.

Communicative crosswords

Included in the last section are four communicative crosswords. These are speaking exercises where students complete a half-finished crossword by exchanging clues with a partner. There are two versions of the crossword: A & B. The words which are missing from A are in B, and vice versa. No clues are provided: the students' task is to invent them. This is an excellent exercise for developing linguistic resourcefulness; in having to define words themselves students practise both their legal vocabulary and the important skill of paraphrasing something when they do not know the word for it.

Using Communicative crosswords

Stage 1 – Set-up. Divide the class into two groups - A and B - with up to four students in each group. Give out the crossword: sheet A to group A, sheet B to group B together with a copy of the dictionary. Go through the rules with them. Some answers may consist of more than one word.
Stage 2 - Preparation. The students discuss the words in their groups, exchanging information about the words they know and checking words they do not know in the ***Dictionary of Law***. Circulate, helping with any problems. This is an important stage: some of the vocabulary in the crosswords is quite difficult.
Stage 3 - Activity. Put the students in pairs - one from group A and one from group B. The students help each other to complete the crosswords by giving each other clues.

Make sure students are aware that the idea is to help each other complete the crossword, rather than to produce obscure and difficult clues.

- What's one down?
- *It's a person who buys something*
- A customer?
- *No, it's a customer who buys a service.*
- A client?
- *Yes, that's right.*

A A	B B
A A	B B

Students work in groups, checking vocabulary.

A B	A B
A B	A B

Students work in pairs, co-operating to solve their crosswords

Alternatively, students can work in small groups, each group consisting of two As and two Bs and using the following strategies:

i) defining the word
ii) describing what the item looks like
iii) stating what the item is used for
iv) describing the person's role
v) stating what the opposite of the word is
vi) giving examples
vii) leaving a gap in a sentence for the word
viii) stating what the word sounds like.

Word association 1: missing links

Each of the sets of four words below can be linked by one other word. All the words are related to legal matters. What are the missing words? Write them in the centre of the charts. The first has been done for you as an example.

1.

civil		court
	..........*law*........	
criminal		school

2.

magistrates'		action
	....	
open		order

3.

grand		service
	....	
petty		box

4.

under		work
	....	
service		law

5.

small		form
	....	
legal		back

Based on the **Dictionary of Law**, second edition
ISBN 0-948549-33-5
Peter Collin Publishing Ltd

Word formation: nouns

A fast way to expand your vocabulary is to make sure you know the different forms of the words you learn. Rewrite the sentences below, changing the verbs (which are in **bold**) to nouns. Don't change the meaning of the sentences, but be prepared to make grammatical changes if necessary. For example:

*The prisoner was **interrogated** for three hours.*
*The prisoner's **interrogation** lasted for three hours.*

1. He was **induced** to steal the plans by an offer of a large amount of money.
   The offer of a large amount of money was his ....

2. The terms of the contract will be **enforced**.
   There will be an ....

3. He is **authorized** to act on our behalf.
   He has ....

4. The contract was **rescinded** last year.
   The ....

5. You will be **punished** for hitting the policeman.
   You face ....

6. The newspaper report stated that he had been **prosecuted** for embezzlement.
   His ....

7. The irregularities in share dealings were **investigated**.
   The ....

8. He **inherited** £10,000 from his grandfather.
   His ....

9. The witness **cancelled** today's appointment last week.
   The witness' ....

10. They **argued** with the judge over the relevance of the documents to the case.
    They got into an ....

Based on the **Dictionary of Law**, second edition
ISBN 0-948549-33-5
Peter Collin Publishing Ltd

Latin pair-up

Many Latin expressions are used in British law, for example *corpus delicti* is the proof that a crime has been committed. Match words from the two boxes, A and B, to make 15 legal expressions which fit the definitions in the list. Each expression should consist of a word from Box A followed by a word from Box B. The first one has been done for you as an example.

Box A

~~BONA~~ CAVEAT COMPOS DOLI HABEAS INTER INTER IPSO OBITER PER PRIMA SUI TOTIES VICE VIVA

Box B

ALIA CAPAX CAPITA CORPUS DICTA EMPTOR FACIE FACTO ~~FIDE~~ GENERIS MENTIS QUOTIES VERSA VIVOS VOCE

Definition	Answer
1. In good faith	bona fide
2. Among other things	
3. The buyer is responsible for checking a	
4. Things which are said in passing	
5. In the opposite way	
6. By speaking	
7. Sane	
8. In a class of its own	
9. As often as necessary	
10. Between living people	
11. A legal remedy against wrongful imprisonment	
12. By this fact, in itself	
13. Capable of crime	
14. For each person	
15. As things seem at first	

Extension. Find three more Latin expressions in the *Dictionary of Law* and teach them to other students in the class.

Based on the **Dictionary of Law**, second edition
ISBN 0-948549-33-5
Peter Collin Publishing Ltd

Word-building

Plural formation

In *Column A* of this table there are 20 nouns relating to legal matters. For each of the nouns decide whether the correct plural form is in *Column B* or *Column C* and then circle it.

The first question has been done for you as an example.

	Column A	*Column B*	*Column C*
1.	referendum	referendums	(referenda)
2.	preservation order	preservations order	preservation orders
3.	bureau	bureaus	bureaux
4.	criterion	criteria	criterions
5.	policewoman	policewomans	policewomen
6.	misdemeanour	misdemeanours	misdemeanoures
7.	corpus	corpora	corpuses
8.	notary public	notary publics	notaries public
9.	memorandum	memoranda	memorandums
10.	juryman	jurymen	jurymans
11.	rejoinder	rejoinders	rejoinderi
12.	moratorium	moratoriums	moratoria
13.	appendix	appendixes	appendices
14.	injunction	injunctions	injuncta
15.	provision	provisiones	provisions
16.	corrigendum	corrigenda	corrigendums
17.	president-elect	presidents-elect	president-elects
18.	LJ	LJJ	LJs
19.	quango	quangi	quangos
20	dictum	dicta	dictums

Based on the **Dictionary of Law**, second edition
ISBN 0-948549-33-5
Peter Collin Publishing Ltd

Word formation: adjectives

The italicised words in the sentences in ***Column A*** are all nouns. What are the adjective forms? Complete the sentences in ***Column B*** using the correct adjective forms.

The first question has been done for you as an example.

	Column A	*Column B*
1.	The company was declared to be in a state of *insolvency*.	The company was declared to be ...*insolvent*....
2.	The jury returned a verdict of not guilty by reason of *insanity*.	The jury found the accused to be .... and not guilty.
3.	He admitted his *guilt*.	He admitted he was ....
4.	His *incompetence* to sign the contract was pointed out.	It was pointed out that he was .... to sign the contract.
5.	There is no *responsibility* on the company's part for loss of customers' property.	The company is not .... for loss of customers' property.
6.	The police found the youth to be in a state of *intoxification*.	The police found the youth to be ....
7.	The solicitor confirmed the *fitness* of her client to plead.	The solicitor confirmed that her client was .... to plead.
8.	Non profit-making organizations can claim tax *exemption*.	Non profit-making organizations are .... from tax.
9.	There is doubt about the *legality* of the company's action in dismissing him.	There is doubt about whether the company's action in dismissing him is completely ....
10.	The court doubted the *legitimacy* of his claim.	The court doubted whether his claim was ....

Based on the **Dictionary of Law**, second edition
ISBN 0-948549-33-5
Peter Collin Publishing Ltd

Word association 2: partnerships

Exercise 1. Link each ***verb*** on the left with a ***noun*** on the right to make ten 'partnerships'.

The first question has been done for you as an example.

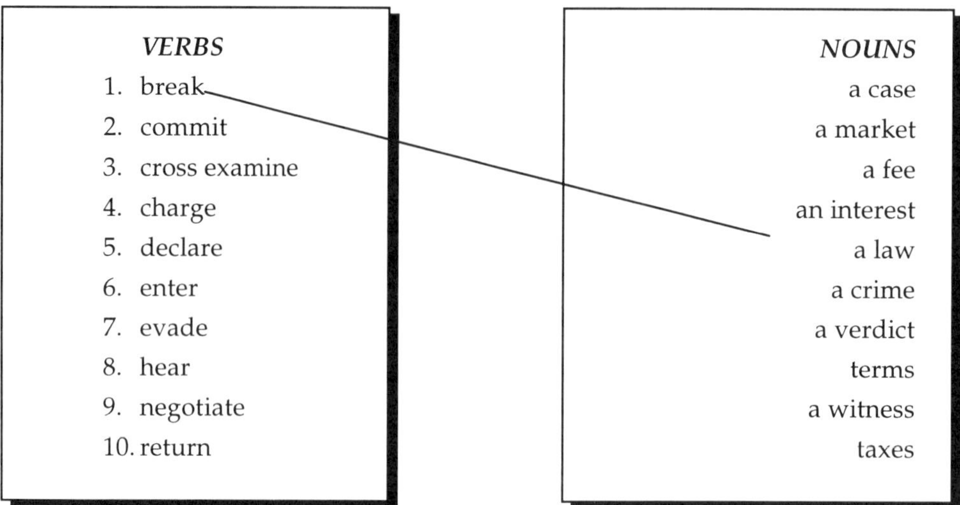

Exercise 2. Complete these sentences using the partnerships from the first exercise. You may have to make some changes to fit the grammar of the sentences. The first one has been done for you as an example.

1. You must know that you are *breaking the law* when you park on the pavement.
2. The merger will only go ahead if the two companies can ______________________ they are both happy with.
3. After two hours' deliberation the jury ______________________ of not guilty.
4. We are going to ______________________ with a revolutionary new product next month.
5. A good accountant can save you money by finding ways to ______________________ .
6. We have ______________________ for the prosecution, which depends on an unreliable identification.
7. When she was ______________________ he contradicted his earlier testimony.
8. I am innocent; I did not ______________________ you accuse me of.
9. During the recent debate on this matter Mr Allen failed to ______________________: he is a director of the company bidding for the contract.
10. Most solicitors do not ______________________ for the first consultation.

Based on the **Dictionary of Law**, second edition
ISBN 0-948549-33-5
Peter Collin Publishing Ltd

Opposites 1: prefixes

Exercise 1. English often uses prefixes to create opposites. There are several different prefixes which are used. Choose the right prefix for each of the adjectives below and write them into the table.

The first question has been done for you: evidence which is *inadmissible* will not be accepted (admitted) by a court.

~~admissible~~ capable valid competent

reliable confirmed correct insured just lawful legal legitimate moral perfect

solvent professional proper reconcilable recoverable regular

dependent movable relevant sane

il-	im-	in-	ir-	un-
1.	1.	1. *inadmissible*	1.	1.
2.	2.	2.	2.	2.
	3.	3.	3.	3.
	4.	4.	4.	4.
		5.		5.
		6.		6.
		7.		
		8.		

Exercise 2. Use 12 of the adjectives in the table to complete these sentences. The first one has been done for you as an example.

1. Hearsay evidence - evidence which a witness has heard from another source — is *inadmissible* in a court of law.
2. Can you check these accounts? Some of the figures seem to be ________________.
3. The witness was completely ________________ : she kept changing her story.
4. It is ________________ for a lawyer to enter into personal relations with a client.
5. We returned the goods to the supplier because they were ________________.
6. That's very interesting, but ________________ : can you please comment only on this case?
7. There are rumours of a takeover, but they are still ________________.
8. It is ________________ to sell tobacco without a licence.
9. The company could not pay its debts and was declared ________________.
10. This document is ________________ without the signature of a witness.
11. The director of the company has left the country permanently and I'm afraid the debt is now ________________.
12. At 21 she left home and became ________________.

ISBN 0-948549-33-5
Peter Collin Publishing Ltd

Word-building

Word formation: verbs

Exercise 1. The words listed in the table below are nouns. What are the verb forms of these nouns?

The first question has been done for you as an example.

1.	abrogation	*to abrogate*	13.	exclusion
2.	abstention		14.	immigration
3.	adjournment		15.	incitement
4.	brief		16.	justification
5.	confinement		17.	misappropriation
6.	corroboration		18.	poll
7.	cross-examination		19.	prosecution
8.	decision		20.	provocation
9.	declaration		21.	representation
10.	deferment		22.	termination
11.	discrimination		23.	veto
12.	embezzlement		24.	violation

Exercise 2. Choose ten verbs from Exercise 1 and write a sentence below for each one. Write the correct form of each verb in the column on the right and leave gaps for the verbs in the sentences. Cover up the right-hand column and give the sentences to another student as a test. For example:

The council has .... the planning regulations.	*violated*

1. ....

2. ....

3. ....

4. ....

5. ....

6. ....

7. ....

8. ....

9. ....

10. ....

Based on the **Dictionary of Law**, second edition
ISBN 0-948549-33-5
Peter Collin Publishing Ltd

Word association 3: mind maps

A mind map is a way of organising vocabulary to show the connections between words. This mind map is based on the word 'theft'.

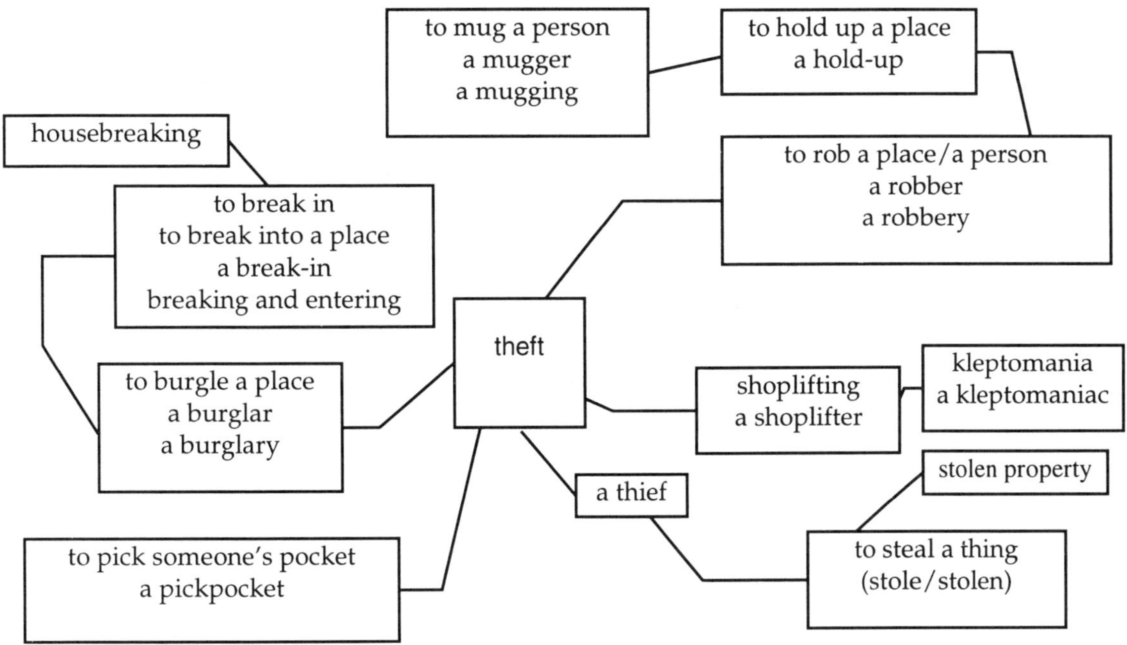

Exercise 1. Find words in the mind map which fit these definitions.

1. The past participle of the verb steal
2. A person who enters a house to steal things
3. To steal something from a person's pocket without him or her noticing
4. To stop a person on the street and using violence or threats to rob him or her
5. Going into a building by force to steal things (one word)
6. A person who steals from a shop
7. A psychological compulsion to steal things
8. A person who commits an act of theft
9. To rob a place, usually by using with guns or other weapons
10. Things obtained by robbery

Exercise 2. Design a mind map for one or more of the following:

- the stock exchange
- tax
- the courtroom

Based on the **Dictionary of Law**, second edition
ISBN 0-948549-33-5
Peter Collin Publishing Ltd

Nouns: name the crime 1

The box below gives the names of 22 crimes. The list gives the definitions of the same crimes. Match the crimes to their definitions. The first one has been done for you: the crime of *assault* is "acting in such a way as to make someone believe he or she will be hurt".

arson assassination ~~assault~~ bigamy blackmail bribery burglary embezzlement espionage extortion forgery fraud libel manslaughter murder perjury piracy robbery slander smuggling theft treason

1. *assault* acting in such a way as to make someone believe he or she will be hurt
2. betraying your country to a foreign power
3. copying patented inventions or copyrighted works
4. entering a building illegally and stealing things
5. getting money from people by threatening to publicise facts they do not want revealed
6. getting money from people by using threats
7. getting property or money from people by making them believe untrue things
8. going through a ceremony of marriage when you are still married to someone else
9. killing a public figure illegally and intentionally
10. killing someone illegally and intentionally
11. killing someone unintentionally or in mitigating circumstances
12. making an illegal copy of a banknote or document
13. offering money corruptly to get someone to do something to help you
14. saying something which damages someone's character
15. setting fire to a building
16. stealing something by using force or threatening to use force
17. stealing, taking property which belongs to someone else
18. taking goods illegally into or out of a country
19. telling lies when you have sworn an oath to say what is true in court
20. trying to find out secrets by illegal means
21. using illegally or stealing money which you are looking after for someone else
22. writing, publishing or broadcasting a statement which damages someone's character

Extension. Work with a partner and test each other. One person turns the page over, while the other asks questions such as *"What do you call the crime of acting in such a way as to make someone believe he or she will be hurt?"* and *"Define 'treason'."*

Based on the **Dictionary of Law**, second edition
ISBN 0-948549-33-5
Peter Collin Publishing Ltd

Nouns: politics

There are 15 words connected with politics in the box below. Use them to complete the sentences — in some cases you will need to make them plural. The first one has been done for you as an example.

abstentions budget consensus ~~constitution~~ devolution houses leader leak

legislation membership policy poll recess spokesman veto

1. Germany has a federal *constitution*.
2. A government ______________ revealed that discussions had been concluded on the treaty.
3. According to the latest opinion ______________ the Prime Minister is more unpopular than ever.
4. Austria's application for ______________ of the EU was successful.
5. Many Scots would like to see more ______________ of power from Westminster.
6. Parliament has introduced ______________ to control the sale of drugs.
7. The bill was passed by both ______________ and sent to the President for signature.
8. The crisis happened during the summer ______________ and Parliament had to be recalled.
9. The government is investigating the latest ______________ of documents relating to the spy trial.
10. The government is running a tight monetary ______________ to try to control inflation.
11. The ______________ of the opposition criticised the Prime Minister for his failure to act.
12. The motion was carried by 200 votes to 150; there were 60 ______________.
13. The President has the power of ______________ over bills passed by Congress.
14. There is a ______________ between all the major parties about what we should do now.
15. The minister has put forward a ______________ aimed at slowing down the economy.

Based on the **Dictionary of Law**, second edition
ISBN 0-948549-33-5
Peter Collin Publishing Ltd

Nouns: name the crime 2

Below are ten statements by defendants. Read the statements and say what crime each one has been accused of.

1. "I arrived home late and found that I'd forgotten my keys. I didn't want to wake my wife up, and I saw there was a ladder in the garden of the house next door . I got the ladder and climbed in. We've just moved house and I didn't realise I was in the wrong street..."

2. "I was walking my dog when I saw the gun lying on the ground. I picked it up - it was still warm - and at that moment I saw the body lying in the long grass. I went across to look and it was my business partner. That's when the police arrived..."

3. "I opened the bank account in a false name as a way to help my employer pay less tax- It's perfectly legal. I kept meaning to tell him, but somehow I just forgot. I bought the villa in France with my own money. It was an inheritance..."

4. "OK, so there are 123 copies of the video. That's perfectly true, but I had no intention of selling them. I'm a collector."

5. "Well this obviously isn't my suitcase. I've never seen these things before in my life. The monogram? Well, they are my initials, but that must be a coincidence. That's probably how the two cases got mixed up. After all, JA aren't very unusual initials. A photograph with me in it? My word, that's incredible! It must be someone who knows me..."

6. "I didn't know my wife was still alive, I thought she'd died in a car accident. I couldn't believe it when I saw her walk into the room. Surely you don't think I married you just to get your money...?"

7. "You misunderstand me. When I offered him the money I meant it as a gift. I know that life can be difficult for a young man on a police salary, especially if he has a family, young children etcetera. It isn't easy and I know that. I just wanted to help. I didn't expect him to do anything in return..."

8. "After leaving the office I realised I'd forgotten my umbrella. I went back in to get it. When I went in I noticed that the photocopier was still turned on. It had been working very badly all day, and I decided to quickly see what was wrong with it before going home. I made a few test copies of documents that were in the office;. I didn't even look at what I was copying. The machine seemed to be working much better. I put the copies in my briefcase — intending to use the other side as notepaper. I don't believe in wasting paper. At that moment Mr Sanders came out of his office..."

9. "I painted them for pleasure. I had no intention of deceiving people. I never said they were by other people. Yes, I did include the signatures of other artists but that's because I wanted them to be perfect copies..."

10. "Mr Wills sent me the money to help me in my business venture — I'm trying to start a design agency. He sent me cheques every month for $1200. A couple of times he sent extra when I had special expenses. It was always understood that he would participate in the profits of the business when it was running. We didn't write anything down, it was an oral agreement, The photographs I have of him with his secretary have no connection with these payments."

Extension. Write a defence for another crime and show it to other students in your class. See if they can guess what crime you are thinking of.

Based on the **Dictionary of Law**, second edition
ISBN 0-948549-33-5
Peter Collin Publishing Ltd

Adjectives 1

All the adjectives in the box are connected with legal matters. Use them to complete the sentences.

The first question has been done for you: a *preliminary hearing* is held before a court case to determine if the whole case should be tried or just some issues.

bankrupt civil concurrent consecutive exemplary exempt flagrant germane hostile intentional joint liable out-of-court overdue ~~preliminary~~

1. After the *preliminary* hearing the judge decided that it was not necessary to try the whole case.
2. Although it was her first case, her conduct of it was ______________ and she was complimented by the judge.
3. As chairman he was personally ______________ for the company's debts.
4. Before leaving the country, the husband took all the money from their ______________ bank account.
5. Giant Inc has offered £500,000 compensation and they are hoping to reach an ______________ settlement this week.
6. He was given two ______________ jail sentences of six months in December, so he will be free by June at the latest.
7. He will obviously be found guilty, it is a ______________ case of corruption.
8. His business was unsuccessful and after only two years he was ______________ .
9. Interest payments on the debt are three weeks ______________ and must be paid immediately.
10. Mr and Mrs Lewes brought a ______________ action against the airline for ruining their holiday.
11. Non-profit making organisations are ______________ from tax.
12. The defendant's wife was ruled a ______________ witness by the judge and cross-examined by the defence.
13. The prosecution claimed that their abusive treatment of the child was an act of ______________ cruelty and not simply the result of a momentary passion.
14. They were given two ______________ jail sentences of two years, so they will be in prison for up to four years.
15. Your argument is not ______________ to the motion and I suggest we return to the business in hand.

Based on the **Dictionary of Law**, second edition
ISBN 0-948549-33-5
Peter Collin Publishing Ltd

Adjectives 2

All the adjectives in the box are connected with legal matters. Use them to complete the sentences.

The first question has been done for you.

biased competent conditional domestic dual equal final ~~guilty~~ heavy legal official ostensible reciprocal unlimited wilful

1. They had the motive, the means and the opportunity — they're obviously _guilty_ .
2. She has ________________ nationality: her parents are Irish but she was born in Italy.
3. It was a serious case and the looters received a ________________ sentence.
4. On investigation we discovered that his ________________ partner had no official connection with the business.
5. I am afraid that this court is not ________________ to deal with this matter. You will have to go to a higher court.
6. Perhaps you do not agree with the company's actions, but they were perfectly ________________ .
7. Of course, you must understand that all this is ________________ on your accepting our price.
8. Money is no problem: the bank has given us ________________ credit.
9. There is no excuse for this; you knew what you were doing: it is a case of ________________ misconduct.
10. The company has not previously exported anything: we have only served the ________________ market.
11. You'll never win the case with this judge — he's completely ________________ against you.
12. The agreement would be ________________: if you sold in our market we would expect the same rights in your market.
13. It must be an ________________ statement; it's signed by the Prime Minister.
14. This month, after 25 years, I will make the ________________ payment and the house will be mine.
15. The law now states that male and female workers must have ________________ pay.

Based on the **Dictionary of Law**, second edition
ISBN 0-948549-33-5
Peter Collin Publishing Ltd

Verbs

All the verbs in the box relate to legal matters. Use them to complete the sentences.

The first question has been done for you as an example.

adjourn	approve	arbitrate	bribe	dismiss	earn	employ	evict	issue	obligate
~~reach~~	recommend	rescind	testify	withhold					

1. The jury was unable to ___reach___ a unanimous decision.
2. The new landlord has started proceedings to ____________ all the tenants.
3. I am sure the board will ____________ your proposal: it's just the sort of thing they're looking for at the moment.
4. The policeman warned him that it was illegal to ____________ evidence.
5. How much dividend do these shares ____________ ?
6. The minister was desperate and even tried to ____________ the policeman to get the charges dropped.
7. Unfortunately the committee has had to ____________ its earlier decision on the use of local government premises.
8. This tribunal will now ____________ until tomorrow at 10 a.m.
9. How many people does the company ____________ ?
10. Are you ready to ____________ in court that this is what happened ?
11. The company is going public and they are going to ____________ 25,000 shares.
12. Do you realise that this contract will ____________ you to buy a minimum quantity of goods each year?
13. This evidence is hearsay and I call upon the court to ____________ it.
14. The prisoner's behaviour has been good and I am going to ____________ him for parole.
15. The management and the union could not agree and they called in an industrial tribunal to ____________ .

Based on the **Dictionary of Law**, second edition
ISBN 0-948549-33-5
Peter Collin Publishing Ltd

Verbs: past tense ~ regular verbs

All the verbs in the box relate to legal matters. Use the past tense forms to complete the sentences.

The first question has been done for you as an example.

accuse	acquit	arrest	award	~~confess~~	charge	drop	engage	fine	grant
imprison	plead	release	seize	serve					

1. After six hours of questioning the accused man _confessed_.
2. The government _______________ an amnesty to all political prisoners.
3. Her boss _______________ her of stealing £250.
4. The secret police _______________ him for six months in a high security jail.
5. We _______________ the best commercial lawyer we could find to represent us but we still lost the case.
6. The prisoner _______________ guilty to all charges.
7. On 12 August they _______________ him with murder.
8. The policeman stopped the car and _______________ the driver.
9. The president _______________ the opposition leader from prison.
10. The court _______________ him £2,500 for obtaining money by false pretences.
11. After consideration, the plaintiff _______________ the case against his neighbour.
12. The customs _______________ the shipment of books.
13. He _______________ six months in a local prison.
14. The Crown Court _______________ the plaintiff £75,000 in damages plus costs.
15. Two of the men were sent to prison, but the judge _______________ the third.

Based on the **Dictionary of Law**, second edition
ISBN 0-948549-33-5
Peter Collin Publishing Ltd

Verbs: mixed tenses 1

All the verbs in the box relate to legal matters. Use them to complete the sentences. You may have to change the forms of the verbs to fit the grammar of the sentences. (Remember the five forms of English verbs, for example: take; takes; took; taken; taking.)

The first question has been done for you as an example.

advise	appeal	commit	~~disclaim~~	disclose	embezzle	establish	follow	impose
legislate	manipulate	offer	preclude	prevent	value			

1. He *disclaimed* all knowledge of the robbery until £250,000 in cash was found in his house.
2. He is ______________ us £100,000 for the house, which is £10,000 less than we wanted.
3. He says he's innocent and he's going to ______________ to the supreme court against the decision.
4. He was sent to prison for six months for ______________ his clients' money.
5. I believe that they are ______________ the accounts to make the company look more profitable.
6. In my opinion they'll ______________ the business at about £2m.
7. Our solicitor has ______________ us to take the documents to the police.
8. Parliament has ______________ against the sale of drugs.
9. The bank has no right to ______________ details of my account to the tax office.
10. The business was ______________ in 1881.
11. The court has ______________ the precedent set in the 1972 case.
12. The magistrate ______________ a fine of £150.
13. The gang had ______________ six robberies before they were caught.
14. They have changed the locks on the building to ______________ the former managing director from going in.
15. This agreement does not ______________ further agreements between these parties in the future.

Based on the **Dictionary of Law**, second edition
ISBN 0-948549-33-5
Peter Collin Publishing Ltd

Verbs: mixed tenses 2

All the verbs in the box relate to legal matters. Use them to complete the sentences. You may have to change the forms of the verbs to fit the grammar of the sentences. The first one has been done for you as an example.

arrange	blackmail	convict	corroborate	exonerate	find	forfeit	infringe	overturn
prohibit	promise	recover	~~refrain~~	sentence	sue			

1. He was asked to give an undertaking to *refrain* from political activity.
2. My client intends to appeal and I am sure that a higher court will ____________ this sentence.
3. I can ____________ Mr Waterman's alibi. At the time of the theft I saw him in Brighton.
4. The judge ____________ him to three years' imprisonment.
5. After the accident he ____________ the company for £50,000 in damages.
6. She was ____________ of manslaughter and sent to prison for eight years.
7. If you decide not to buy you will ____________ your 25% deposit.
8. The court has ____________ him guilty on all charges.
9. We believe that this production ____________ our copyright as detailed below.
10. The company went out of business and the original investment was never ____________ .
11. We discovered that his secretary was ____________ him with certain details about his private life.
12. You ____________ to pay by August and it's now September. What's your explanation?
13. The law ____________ the sale of alcohol to minors.
14. All the files are ____________ in alphabetical order, so it's very easy to find.
15. The judge ____________ the driver from all responsibility for the accident.

Based on the **Dictionary of Law**, second edition
ISBN 0-948549-33-5
Peter Collin Publishing Ltd

Phrasal verbs 1

Phrasal verbs are common in conversational English. Match each phrasal verb below with its correct definition.

The first question has been done for you as an example.

Phrasal verb	*Definition*
1. break down	a. to start to do something in place of someone else, (ii) to buy a company
2. break in	b. to divide (a company) into separate units
3. break off	c. to invest
4. break up	d. to pretend something is not what it is to cheat a customer
5. bring forward	e. to go into a building by force in order to steal
6. bring in	f. to trick, to deceive
7. bring up	g. to stop because of failure
8. call in	h. to pay as a deposit
9. hand down	i. to change to an earlier date
10. hold up	j. (i) to end a meeting, (ii) to put a company into liquidation
11. pass off	k. to refer to something for the first time
12. put down	l. to decide a verdict
13. put into	m. to ask someone to come to help
14. take in	n. to give to the next generation through inheritance
15. take over	o. (i) to rob from a bank or vehicle using weapons, (ii) to stay at a high level, (iii) to delay
16. wind up	p. to stop a discussion or negotiation

Extension. Work with a partner. Test each other: one person closes the book, the other asks questions. For example: *"Tell me a verb which means 'to divide a company into separate units'."*

Based on the **Dictionary of Law**, second edition
ISBN 0-948549-33-5
Peter Collin Publishing Ltd

Phrasal verbs 2

Use the phrasal verbs from the previous page to complete the sentences. You will have to use some verbs more than once, and you may have to change the form of the verb to fit the grammar of the sentence.

The first question has been done for you as an example.

1. The company ACT has been *broken up* into seven autonomous divisions.
2. He had a factory which manufactured cheap sports clothes which he ___________ ___________ as high-quality designer goods.
3. He ___________ all of us ___________ with his promise of quick profits and low risks.
4. He was caught ___________ ___________ to a clothes shop at night.
5. He ___________ ___________ the meeting with a vote of thanks to the chairman.
6. I'm very busy on Wednesday: can I___________ our meeting ___________ to Tuesday?
7. John is leaving in June and there will be a gap of one month before the new manager ___________ ___________ .
8. Management and unions could not agree and negotiations ___________ ___________ at midnight yesterday.
9. Payment will be ___________ ___________ until the contract is signed.
10. Shares in ACT have increased in price by 35 pence with the news that they are to be ___________ ___________ by Giant PLC .
11. The car was still under guarantee when it ___________ ___________ .
12. The company was insolvent and the court ordered it to be ___________ ___________ .
13. The share price ___________ ___________ well through the summer and then fell in September.
14. They are accused of ___________ ___________ a security van and stealing £45,000.
15. This watch was ___________ ___________ to me from my great-grandfather.
16. When he lost his job he ___________ his savings ___________ opening a design studio.
17. The chairman ___________ ___________ the question of corruption in the police force.
18. You have to ___________ £200 ___________ now and then pay £100 a month for 18 months.
19. The jury ___________ ___________ a verdict of not guilty.
20. The local police decided to ___________ ___________ the CID to help in the murder hunt.

Based on the **Dictionary of Law**, second edition
ISBN 0-948549-33-5
Peter Collin Publishing Ltd

Verbs: active/passive

Change the sentences below from active to passive tense. For example:
Active: *The policeman asked for proof of identification.*
Passive: *Proof of identification was asked for by the policeman.*

Remember that it is not always necessary to mention the *subject* in a passive sentence. For example:
Active: *In this instance we overlooked the delay.*
Passive: *In this instance the delay was overlooked.*

1. The constable arrested the driver of the stolen car.

   Passive: ....

2. The judge asked the witness to write the name on a piece of paper.

   Passive: ....

3. The company is going to issue a writ to prevent the trade union from going on strike.

   Passive: ....

4. He wrote his will in 1990.

   Passive: ....

5. The pleading itemizes the damage.

   Passive: ....

6. My grandmother left £5,000 to me in her will.

   Passive: ....

7. The court granted the company a two-week stay of execution.

   Passive: ....

8. They should call in detectives to help in the murder hunt.

   Passive: ....

9. The applicant is seeking judicial review to quash the order.

   Passive: ....

10. They left the wounded man lying in the road.

   Passive: ....

Based on the **Dictionary of Law**, second edition
ISBN 0-948549-33-5
Peter Collin Publishing Ltd

Parts of speech

Adverbs

There are adverbs which are typical of legal documents. In fact, some of them are *only* used in legal documents. They are used to refer clearly to specific times and places in and around documents. Most are formed using *here* and *there*.

Here means this document - the one you are reading
There means that document - the one which is being discussed, not the one you are reading

Some adverbs with *here* and *there* are listed below. Match them to the correct definitions.

The first question has been done for you as an example: *hereafter* is used to talk about future time: what will happen after the document is written and signed: *"The house will hereafter be the property of Mr Jackson"*.

Here

1. hereafter	accompanying this document
2. hereby	appearing somewhere in this document
3. herein	following this document
4. hereinafter	in the future - from the production of this document on
5. hereof	listed later in this document
6. hereto	mentioned in this same section of this document
7. heretofore	previous to the production of this document
8. herunder	relating to this document or part of it
9. herewith	resulting from this document

There

1. thereafter	accompanying that document
2. thereby	appearing somewhere in that document
3. therefore	following that document
4. therein	for that reason or purpose
5. thereinafter	from the production of that document until now
6. thereinbefore	in the time before that document was produced
7. thereinunder	listed later in that document
8. thereof	mentioned in that section of that document
9. thereto	mentioned previously in that document
10. theretofore	relating to that document
11. therewith	resulting from that document or decision

Based on the **Dictionary of Law**, second edition
ISBN 0-948549-33-5
Peter Collin Publishing Ltd

Prepositions

The 20 sentences in this exercise contain **mistakes**. The mistakes are all in the prepositions and there are three types.

1. MISSING PREPOSITION	I spoke^him about this last week.	to
2. WRONG PREPOSITION	We're meeting again ~~in~~^Tuesday.	on
3. UNNECESSARY PREPOSITION	I'll telephone ~~to~~ you tomorrow.	

Find the mistakes and correct them.

1. It says in the newspaper that he's been evading of income tax.
2. The prosecution tried to discredit at the defence witness.
3. I am writing in behalf of Mr and Mrs Smith...
4. I would like to report of a theft.
5. He was awarded £100,000 to compensate of the damages caused by the manufacturer.
6. The directors of the firm were accused insider trading.
7. If you don't tell me you'll be charged to withholding evidence.
8. In view of your failure to pay, I have instructed to my solicitors to start proceedings immediately.
9. We have referred your question at the tribunal and hope to have an answer for you in the next few days.
10. After six months in prison she will be eligible to parole.
11. The next national holiday falls in a Monday.
12. They decided to sue at the landlord for failure to maintain the property.
13. During the appeal he claimed that the original judge had been biased in favour to the plaintiff.
14. The defendant was negligent to carrying out his duties as a trustee.
15. The company was declared to be of a state of insolvency.
16. My client disagrees with clause 6 of the contract which expressly forbids to sales in the USA.
17. The judge ruled that her evidence was inadmissible and it was expunged the report.
18. Does the bill include of VAT or is that extra?
19. The judge acquitted to the husband but imposed a £250 fine on the wife.
20. He was found guilty of all charges and sentenced five years in prison.

Extension. Write three sentences with deliberate mistakes in the prepositions. Check them with the teacher, then show them to a partner to see if he or she can find the mistakes.

Based on the **Dictionary of Law**, second edition
ISBN 0-948549-33-5
Peter Collin Publishing Ltd

Pronunciation

Word stress

All English words with more than one syllable have a stress: one syllable which is emphasised more than the others. There are three possible patterns for three-syllable words. Look at these examples and practise saying them.

1. Stress on the first syllable	❶②③	For example: ***cri**-mi-nal; **occ**-u-pant; **le**-gis-late*
2. Stress on the second syllable	①❷③	For example: *fi-**nan**-cial; co-**llec**-tion; ex-**po**-sure*
3. Stress on the third syllable	①②❸	For example: *le-ga-**tee**; dis-po-**ssess**; con-tra-**vene***

Read the conversations below and find all the three-syllable words. Underline them and classify them in the groups on the right. The first one has been done for you as an example.

Conversation 1

- ● *Have you seen the evidence? It looks very strong.*
- ○ Yes, but we still expect an acquittal.
- ● *Do you really think she's innocent?*
- ○ Wait until you see the forensic report.

Conversation 2

- ● *I hear the Appeal Court disapproved of the decision.*
- ○ Yes, they said that the indictment was incorrect.
- ● *What's Jack's opinion?*
- ○ Oh, he's very upset.

Conversation 3

- ● *Would you recommend buying shares in Giant Plc?*
- ○ No. Their performance has been poor lately. There are better companies.
- ● *For example?*
- ○ I've made a selection for you to consider. Let me give you a copy.

Conversation 4

- ● *Have you heard about Giant? One of their employees embezzled over £200,000 in six months.*
- ○ No. Who was it?
- ● *They don't know yet but it may have been the director of the accounts department.*
- ○ Do you think they'll prosecute?

Conversation 5

- ● *Look at this. Another case of government corruption.*
- ○ Is that the thing about the Minister for the Arts?
- ● *No, it's the Treasury Secretary. He's been accused of insider trading.*
- ○ What are the details?

GROUP 1 ❶②③

1. evidence
2.
3.
4.
5.
6.
7.

GROUP 2 ①❷③

1.
2.
3.
4.
5.
6.
7.
8.
9.
10.
11.
12.
13.
14.

GROUP 3 ①②❸

1.
2.
3.
4.

Extension. Work with a partner and practise the conversations.

Based on the **Dictionary of Law**, second edition
ISBN 0-948549-33-5
Peter Collin Publishing Ltd

Verbs & nouns

Sometimes two words can be spelled the same but pronounced differently. This is often because one word is a noun and the other is a verb. One example is the word 'import':

1. *Oil is a major **im**-port for France.*	NOUN	❶② stress on the first syllable.
1. *Does Britain im-**port** a lot of wine?.*	VERB	①❷ stress on the second syllable.

Read the following sentences. Decide in each case if the word in *italics* is a verb or a noun. Then decide which stress pattern it has and complete the table . The first one has been done for you as an example.

		noun verb	❶②	①❷
1.	France, Spain, Greece and Italy *export* olive oil.	verb		×
2.	Manufactured goods are Japan's principal *export.*			
3.	The main *suspect* in murder the investigation is the husband.			
4.	We *suspect* that the robbery was carried out by someone inside the company.			
5.	Great news: they've offered us the *contract.*			
6.	We're going to *contract* a company called All Clear to deal with security.			
7.	Given the evidence, I'm sure they'll *convict* him.			
8.	He wrote to you from prison - you must have known he was a *convict.*			
9.	I'm sorry, you can't park here without a *permit.*			
10.	This document will *permit* you to sell computer systems abroad.			
11.	It's important to *record* everything the prisoner says during interrogation.			
12.	We keep a *record* of sales from day to day on the computer.			
13.	The *object* of our meeting today is to discuss the damages claim by Mr Larsen.			
14.	I'm told that you *object* to one of the clauses in the agreement.			
15.	With your permission, I would like to read you an *extract* from the statement.			
16.	Can you go through the accounts and *extract* the information he's asking for?			
17.	The two companies will *conduct* negotiations which may lead to a merger.			
18.	She divorced him because of his unreasonable *conduct.*			
19.	I don't *dispute* your claim to the estate.			
20.	I believe there is a *dispute* between my client and yours.			

Based on the **Dictionary of Law**, second edition
ISBN 0-948549-33-5
Peter Collin Publishing Ltd

Pronunciation

Present simple

In the third person of the present simple, the verb adds an 's' at the end: *I walk, he walks*. There are three different pronunciations of the 's'. Look at the examples and practise saying them.

1. /s/	like the sound in *sue*	For example:	*convicts; keeps; checks*
2. /z/	like the sound in *zero*	For example:	*tries; opens; sells*
3. / Iz/	like the sound in *prison*	For example:	*accuses; witnesses; publishes*

Find the third person present simple verbs in these sentences and underline them. Decide which of the three pronunciations is correct in each case.

The first question has been done for you as an example.

	❶ /s/	❷ /z/	❸ /Iz/
1. Sometimes the accused pleads guilty in the hope of reducing the sentence.		×	
2. This information certainly helps the case for the defendant.			
3. If the judge dismisses the evidence we'll object.			
4. Often a higher court commutes the death sentence to one of life imprisonment.			
5. She's the director of an agency which collects debts for other companies.			
6. According to this document, Mrs Winter claims £10,000 for damages to her home.			
7. The contractor discharges the contract only when all works are completed.			
8. He leases office space from a large property company.			
9. On these grounds my client repudiates this contract.			
10. This document summarises the events leading to the raid on the house.			
11. Being a judge disqualifies you from being a Member of Parliament.			
12. Sometimes a court acquits someone who is guilty.			
13. This letter corroborates the accused's alibi.			
14. We need to know if the company intends to sue for damages.			
15. Our legal advisor recommends that we do not apply for an injunction.			
16. My client owns a publishing company in Brazil.			
17. The committee discriminates between proposals on grounds of community benefit.			
18. This company employs more than 5,000 people in 16 countries.			
19. We have a department which assesses property for the purposes of insurance.			
20. The government taxes this type of transaction at 8%.			
21. After he signs he won't be able to change his mind again.			
22. The next national holiday falls on a Monday.			
23. Some people feel that the arrival of multinationals corrupts local bureaucrats.			
24. The family still controls the business.			
25. Our lawyer advises us that we can sue if we wish to.			

Extension. The same rule applies to plurals: /s/ clerks; /z/ lawyers; /Iz/ judges. Work with a partner and think of five nouns in each pronunciation category.

Based on the **Dictionary of Law**, second edition
ISBN 0-948549-33-5
Peter Collin Publishing Ltd

Past tense & past participle

Pronunciation

Regular past tenses and past participles are formed with the suffix 'ed': *walk, walked, walked.* There are three different pronunciations of the 'ed' at the end of the verb. Look at these examples and practise saying them.

1.	/t/	like the sound in *trial*	For example:	*expressed; tricked; helped*
2.	/d/	like the sound in *dock*	For example:	*accused; opened; claimed*
3.	/Id/	like the sound in *bid*	For example:	*convicted; pleaded; acquitted*

Find the regular past tense verbs in these sentences and underline them. Decide which of the three pronunciations is correct in each case. The first one has been done for you as an example.

	❶ /t/	❷ /d/	❸ /Id/
1. The clerk was disciplined for leaking the report to a newspaper.		×	
2. He claims he was discriminated against because of his colour.			
3. The company is presumed to be still solvent.			
4. The market has not recovered from the rise in oil prices.			
5. The legislation was reformed to make court room procedure more straightforward.			
6. The letters were despatched today.			
7. The contract becomes null and void when these documents are surrendered.			
8. He was blackmailed by his former secretary.			
9. His firm was blacklisted by the government.			
10. He promised to pay the money before the end of the month.			
11. The gang swindled the bank out of £1.5m.			
12. He practised as a solicitor for 25 years			
13. The defendant is represented by his solicitor.			
14. The company has recorded another year of increased sales.			
15. The court adjourned to allow the prosecution time to find the missing witnesses.			
16. The recession caused hundreds of bankruptcies.			
17. The judge sentenced him to two years in prison.			
18. The political prisoners were pardoned by the president.			
19. He traded under the name 'Eeziphitt'.			
20. He was summoned to appear before the committee.			
21. The new building must be financed by the local authority.			
22. We based our calculations on last year's turnover			
23. The government has not published the figures.			
24. The agent is empowered to sell the property.			
25. The judge decided in favour of the plaintiff.			

Based on the **Dictionary of Law**, second edition
ISBN 0-948549-33-5
Peter Collin Publishing Ltd

Multiple meanings

Some words have more than one meaning. For example a *party* is a person involved in a legal dispute (*"One of the parties to the dispute has died"*) but it is also a political organisation (*"Lincoln was a member of the Republican party"*). Can you identify the following eight words? Two or three meanings are given for each word.

1. This word means:
    - a meeting or a series of meetings: *"There is a Democratic _____ in August:"*
    - an international treaty: *"All the countries agreed to a new arms _____."*
    - the way something is usually done: *"We have a ____ that the President enters first."*

2. This word means:
    - money invested or borrowed: *"You don't pay off the _____ until the end of the loan period."*
    - A person or company represented by agents: *"The agent has come to London to see his _____"*
    - person responsible for something: *"Whose name appears on the contract as _____ ?"*

3. This word means:
    - something which is for sale: *"This _____ is very attractively priced."*
    - a section of a legal agreement: *"If you look at _____ 7 of the contract you'll see why."*

4. This word means:
    - an area of land: *"The _____ is 100 square kilometres."*
    - property left by a dead person: *"His _____ was worth $1.5m."*

5. This word means:
    - proper, correct: *"We will not release the documents without _____ procedure being followed."*
    - owed: *"The next payment is _____ on the 5th of October."*
    - expected to arrive: *"He isn't _____ until seven o'clock."*

6. This word means:
    - to say something clearly: *"I _____ now that my client is completely innocent."*
    - independent country: *"All citizens have obligations to the _____."*

7. This word means:
    - special attention: *"I took a particular _____ in this case."*
    - money paid for the use of money: *"What is the current rate of _____?"*
    - ownership of shares in a company: *"He has a majority _____ in a newspaper."*

8. This word means:
    - to put into words or diagrams: *"You must _____ the idea more clearly."*
    - very fast: *"I'll send the papers to you _____ delivery."*

Based on the **Dictionary of Law**, second edition
ISBN 0-948549-33-5
Peter Collin Publishing Ltd

Test your criminal slang

How good are you at detective work? Below there are four conversations. These conversations include 14 slang words. The definitions of the words are in the box on the right. Read the conversations, and use the context to match the words to the definitions.

Conversation 1

- ○ *Have you heard about Henry?*
- ● No. What?
- ○ *He's been nicked.*
- ● You're joking. What happened?
- ○ *He was blagging a bank with his brother and somebody grassed on them.*
- ● Who's the nark?
- ○ *Who knows? Henry's got a lot of enemies.*

Conversation 2

- ○ *What did he get?*
- ● Eight years.
- ○ *Eight years inside! I thought you said he had a good brief.*
- ● Well, he thought he did.
- ○ *Where's he going to do it?*
- ● Isle of Wight.
- ○ *Oh no. The screws in there are the worst in the world.*

Conversation 3

- ○ *So, what have you got for me?*
- ● Rolex watches. Two hundred of them.
- ○ *Are they hot?*
- ● What do you think? Would I come to a fence like you with them if they weren't?
- ○ *Leave them with me tonight and I'll give you a price for them in the morning.*
- ● Leave it out. Do I look like a mug?
- ○ *Sorry?*
- ● I'm surprised at you, trying a scam like that. I wasn't born yesterday. I want a price now.

Conversation 4

- ○ *At one time I had 50 people selling heroin in clubs around the city.*
- ● Really? Didn't you have any problem with the law?
- ○ *No, they were all bent in those days. A bit of cash every month and they were happy.*
- ● So why did you open the supermarkets?
- ○ *Originally it was a way to launder the drugs money. In the end it became more interesting to be legitimate.*

Definitions

1. ____________ = a buyer of stolen property
2. ____________ = a lawyer
3. ____________ = a person who is easily deceived
4. ____________ = a prison guard
5. ____________ = a trick
6. ____________ = an informer
7. ____________ = corrupt
8. ____________ = in prison
9. ____________ = stolen
10. ____________ = the police
11. *to nick* = to arrest
12. ____________ = to hold up, to rob using weapons
13. ____________ = to inform the police
14. ____________ = to transfer illegally gained money to a normal bank account

Based on the **Dictionary of Law**, second edition
ISBN 0-948549-33-5
Peter Collin Publishing Ltd

Categories

In this table there are 22 crimes and seven categories of crime. Decide which category each crime belongs to. The first one has been done for you as an example.

	crimes against the person	crimes against property	sexual offences	political offences	offences against justice	public order offences	road traffic offences
burglary		X					
reckless driving							
obscenity							
murder							
theft							
rape							
treason							
breach of the peace							
manslaughter							
criminal damage							
buggery							
abduction							
bigamy							
perjury							
robbery							
assault							
blackmail							
grievous bodily harm							
forgery							
battery							
sedition							
peverting the course of justice							

Based on the **Dictionary of Law**, second edition
ISBN 0-948549-33-5
Peter Collin Publishing Ltd

Odd one out

In each of the following sets of four, one word or expression is the *odd one out:* different from the others. Find the word that is different and circle it. For example:

lawyer .... *judge* .... *criminal* .... *policeman*

Criminal is the odd one out: the other three all defend the law.

1. divorced .... married .... separated .... alone
2. judge .... counsel .... barrister .... solicitor
3. robbery .... arson .... shoplifting .... burglary
4. indict .... accuse .... charge .... convict
5. responsibility .... duty .... right .... obligation
6. murder .... blackmail .... manslaughter .... homicide
7. hereafter .... hereinafter .... hereunder .... herewith
8. collateral .... plea .... surety .... guarantor
9. condemnation .... clemency .... pardon .... mercy
10. guillotine .... electric chair .... gas chamber .... execution
11. dispense .... distribute .... disburse .... discredit
12. ransom .... abduct .... take hostage .... kidnap
13. accidentally .... deliberately .... knowingly .... wilfully
14. verdict .... ruling .... appeal .... decision
15. intellectual property .... royalty .... patent .... copyright
16. joint venture .... partnership .... contract .... merger
17. accused .... witness .... defendant .... prisoner
18. admit .... permit .... allow .... deny

Based on the **Dictionary of Law**, second edition
ISBN 0-948549-33-5
Peter Collin Publishing Ltd

Opposites 2

Exercise 1. The words below are all from the world of law. Match them into 12 pairs of words with opposite meanings and write them in the table. The first one has been done for you as an example: *guilty* and *innocent* are opposites.

accidental
acquit borrow bring forward
cancel civil confess confirm convict
criminal defence defendant defer deliberate deny
~~guilty~~ imprison ~~innocent~~ landlord lend
plaintiff prosecution release
tenant

guilty - innocent		

Exercise 2. Complete these 12 sentences. Use one word from each pair of opposites. The first one has been done for you as an example.

1. He was found ___guilty___ and sentenced to two years in prison.
2. There was insufficient evidence for the court to ______________ her.
3. As the accused was seriously ill, the judge decided to ______________ the trial until the 23rd.
4. The ______________ says he cannot pay the amount the court has awarded.
5. According to the terms of the contract, if the ______________ doesn't pay the rent for two months he can be evicted.
6. The police were accused of using torture to make suspects ______________.
7. Before you ______________ such a large amount of money, are you sure you can repay it?
8. He brought a ______________ action against the company, claiming that the accident had been caused by a manufacturing fault in the automobile.
9. He has served 12 years in prison and the authorities will ______________ him tomorrow.
10. The ______________ case is that the accused could not have committed this crime as he was in Glasgow on the day in question.
11. I'm afraid I'll have to ______________ our meeting on the 16th - I have to go to Berlin on that day to see a client.
12. The question is this: when he left the gun in the room was it a ______________ plan or a moment of carelessness?

Extension. Work with a partner and test each other. One person closes the book, the other asks questions. For example: *"What's the opposite of 'guilty'?"*

Based on the **Dictionary of Law**, second edition
ISBN 0-948549-33-5
Peter Collin Publishing Ltd

Abbreviations

All these abbreviations are connected to the law. How many of them do you know? Write the full versions on the right. The first one has been done for you as an example. "Also known as" is used to give the different names when a criminal or terrorist uses more than one: *"Richard Williams, a.k.a. the Bayswater Bomber".*

1. a.k.a. *also known as* ____________________
2. AOB ____________________
3. c.o.d. ____________________
4. DA ____________________
5. e. & o.e. ____________________
6. e.g. ____________________
7. f.o.b. ____________________
8. FBI ____________________
9. FO ____________________
10. GBH ____________________
11. GNP ____________________
12. ID ____________________
13. Inc ____________________
14. IOU ____________________
15. JP ____________________
16. L/C ____________________
17. MEP ____________________
18. p.p. ____________________
19. PLC ____________________
20. PR ____________________
21. QC ____________________
22. recd ____________________
23. v. ____________________
24. VAT ____________________

ISBN 0-948549-33-5
Peter Collin Publishing Ltd

Who's speaking?

The statements below are all taken from the same case. They were made orally in open court during the trial. Read them and decide who made each statement within the court. For example, the first statement, number 1, was made by the counsel for the prosecution.

1. "I would like to remind you of the testimony of Mrs Ellen Barry. She told us that her husband phoned her to say that he had had a successful day. Now, Mr Barry was a drugs dealer, yet when the police arrived on the scene of the crime he had a total of £12.50 in his pockets. We also know that he had borrowed money from Mr Swan on a previous occasion and failed to repay it."

2. "He was getting angrier by the minute. He said he wasn't going to let me make a fool of him and then he took out a gun. I was astonished. He started waving it around and shouting. I turned to run away and he shot me in the leg."

3. "I apprehended Mr Swan on Standish Lane, a few minutes from the scene of the shooting . At the time of his arrest he had £1,000 and a handgun on his person. He was very distressed, but made no attempt to resist arrest."

4. "I was on my way home from the pub when I saw two men arguing. They seemed to be talking about money. They were very angry and both of them were shouting. I wasn't really listening to be honest. Suddenly I heard a shot. When I looked round one of them was lying on the floor and the other had disappeared."

5. "I went out to the bank at the end of the afternoon to deposit the money in my business account, but I arrived too late and the bank was closed. I kept the money with me when I went out that night,. I didn't want to leave it in the office overnight: we've had a couple of burglaries recently. I was carrying the gun for my own protection. It's licensed. When he attacked me I panicked. It was self-defence."

6. "Mark rang me from the pub at about seven o'clock. He said it had gone very well. I supposed he meant that the deal had gone through. He couldn't tell me on the phone. He said he was going to celebrate and he'd be home late."

7. "Mr Swan let me go home early. He said he was going to close up the office and go round to the bank."

8. "This is a very serious crime, and all the more shocking as it is committed by a man with a comfortable position in society. I find myself with no choice but to sentence you to eight years in prison. Had your victim not survived, which may be due as much to poor marksmanship as compassion, you would have found yourself facing a far longer sentence."

9. "We find the defendant guilty as charged."

10. "You have heard that Mr Barry was a habitual criminal, whereas my client was a respected local businessman. Does it seem to you probable that a respectable person, someone like yourselves, would go out with a gun to collect debts as my learned friend suggests?"

Extension. Can you reconstruct the story of the case from the statements?

Based on the **Dictionary of Law**, second edition
ISBN 0-948549-33-5
Peter Collin Publishing Ltd

The courts

Link the courts in the left-hand column with their definitions on the right by drawing a line between the correct connections. The first one has been done for you as an example.

Court	*Definition*
1. *small claims court*	h. court which deals with disputes over small amounts of money
2. *Court of Appeal*	a. court responsible for settling disputes relating to European Community Law, and also acting as a last Court of Appeal against laws in individual countries
3. *County Court*	b. court presided over by a coroner
4. *European Court of Human Rights*	c. court which hears appeals from industrial tribunals
5. *industrial tribunal*	d. main civil court in England and Wales
6. *magistrates' court*	e. highest court of appeal in both civil and criminal cases in England and Wales
7. *coroner's court*	f. court which decides in disputes involving ships
8. *Crown Court*	g. court which hears local civil cases
9. *Lands Tribunal*	i. civil or criminal court to which a person may go to ask for an award or a sentence to be changed
10. *Judicial Committee of the Privy Council*	j. court considering the rights of citizens of states which are parties to the European Convention for the Protection of Human Rights
11. *Commercial Court*	k. court which can decide in disputes between employers and employees
12. *rent tribunal*	l. court presided over by magistrates
13. *High Court*	m. court which administers the property of people suffering from disability
14. *European Court of Justice*	n. court, formed of a circuit judge and jury, which hears criminal cases
15. *Court of Protection*	o. court which adjudicates in disputes about rent, and can award a fair rent
16. *Employment Appeal Tribunal*	p. appeal court for appeals from courts outside the UK, such as the courts of some Commonwealth countries
17. *Judicial Committee of the House of Lords*	q. court which deals with compensation claims relating to land
18. *Admiralty Court*	r. court in the Queen's Bench division which hears cases relating to business disputes

Based on the **Dictionary of Law**, second edition
ISBN 0-948549-33-5
Peter Collin Publishing Ltd

What am I?

Match the legal roles in ***Column A*** with the descriptions in ***Column B***. The first one has been done for you as an example.

Column A	*Column B*
1. barrister	a. "I am an unpaid official who tries cases in a police court."
2. Lord Chancellor	b. "I am chief magistrate in a magistrates' court."
3. Treasury Solicitor	c. "I sit in the County Courts and the Crown Courts."
4. master	d. "I preside over the Civil Division of the Court of Appeal and am responsible for admitting solicitors to the Roll of Solicitors."
5. magistrate	e. "I am an expert judge appointed by the High Court to try complicated, usually technical, cases where specialist knowledge is required."
6. Lord Chief Justice	f. "I am one of the Law Officers, a Member of Parliament, who prosecutes for the Crown in certain cases, advises government departments on legal problems and decides if major criminal offences should be tried."
7. Lord of Appeal	g. "I am a member of the Government and Cabinet who presides over the debates in the House of Lords and am responsible for the administration of justice and appointment of judges."
8. chairman of the justices	h. "I am a lawyer who can plead or argue a case in one of the higher courts in England."
9. circuit judge	i. "I am an official in the Queen's Bench Division and I examine and decide on preliminary matters before trial."
10. Master of the Rolls	j. "I am the chief judge of the Queen's Bench Division of the High Court and a member of the Court of Appeal."
11. Attorney-General	k. "I am a member of the House of Lords who sits when the House is acting as a Court of Appeal."
12. official referee	l. "I am the solicitor who is head of the Government's legal department in England and Wales and legal adviser to the Cabinet Office and other government departments."

Based on the **Dictionary of Law**, second edition
ISBN 0-948549-33-5
Peter Collin Publishing Ltd

Anagrams 1

Read the definitions and put the letters in order to make 15 words connected with the law. Write the words in the grid to find the mystery phrase. The first anagram has been done for you: an *accomplice* is a person who helps another person perform a criminal act.

1. Criminal's assistant........ ACCCEILMOP
2. Ways in which something is done........ CDEEOPRRSU
3. Money invested or borrowed on which interest is paid........ ACIILNPPR
4. Fair and just for all parties........ ABEEILQTU
5. Wanting or planning to do something........ EIINNNOTT
6. Not permanent........ AEMOPRRTY
7. A date and a time to meet........ AEIMNNOPPTT
8. System for giving money to the government........ AAINOTTX
9. Agreement to lend money to buy a house........ AEGGMORT
10. Postponed, delayed, changed to a later date........ DDEEEFRR
11. The way it was done on an earlier occasion........ CDEEENPRT
12. Not serious........ FILOORSUV
13. Act of occupying a property........ ACCCNOPUY
14. Relating to a company........ ACEOOPRRT
15. The rules of politeness........ EEEIQTTTU

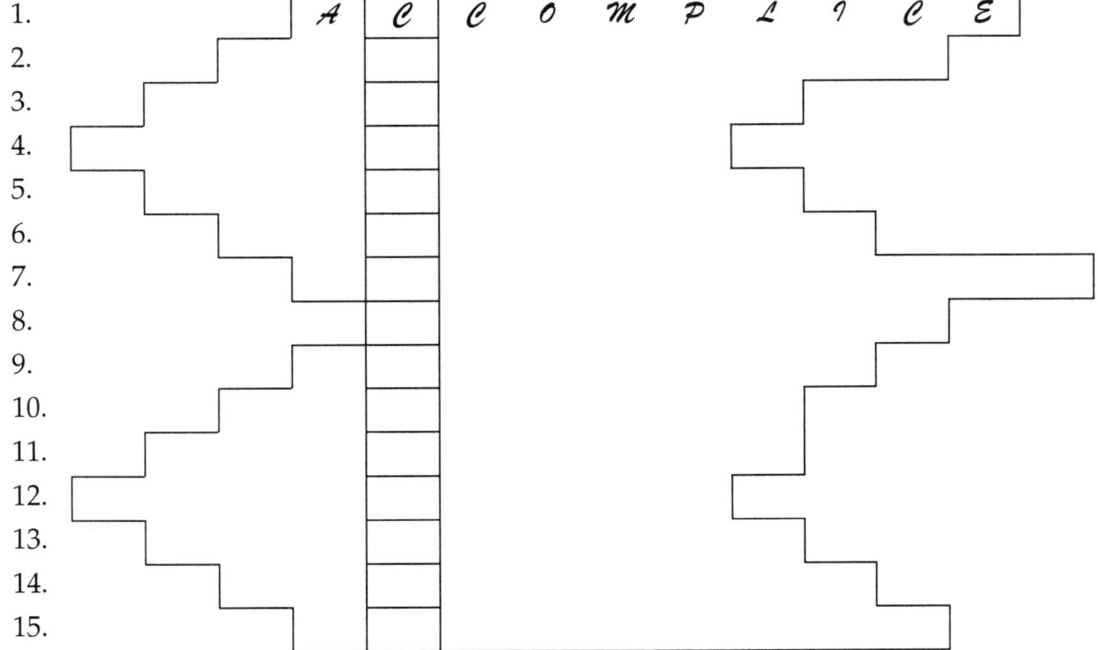

Mystery Phrase: being rude to a court, as by bad behaviour in court, or by refusing to carry out a court order

Based on the **Dictionary of Law**, second edition
ISBN 0-948549-33-5
Peter Collin Publishing Ltd

Communicative crossword 1 sheet A

This crossword is not complete: you have only half the words. The other half are on sheet B. Check that you know the words in your crossword. Then work with a partner who has sheet B to complete the two crosswords. Follow these three rules:

1. Speak only in English
2. Don't say the word in the crossword
3. Don't show your crossword to your partner.

"What's one across?"

→ across, ↓ down

Based on the **Dictionary of Law**, second edition
ISBN 0-948549-33-5
Peter Collin Publishing Ltd

Communicative crossword 1 sheet B

Puzzles & Quizzes

This crossword is not complete: you have only half the words. The other half are on sheet A. Check that you know the words in your crossword. Then work with a partner who has sheet A to complete the two crosswords. Follow these three rules:

1. Speak only in English
2. Don't say the word in the crossword
3. Don't show your crossword to your partner.

"What's one across?"

→ across, ↓ down

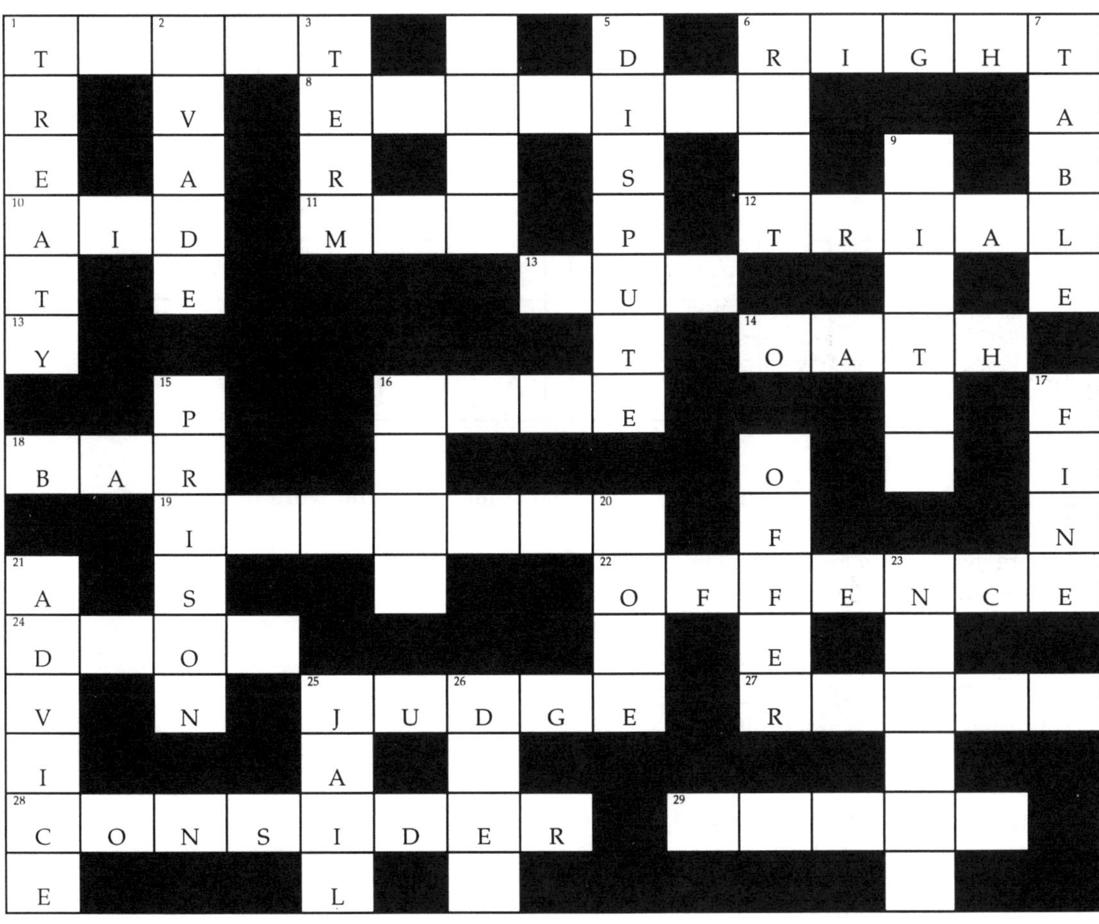

Based on the **Dictionary of Law**, second edition
ISBN 0-948549-33-5
Peter Collin Publishing Ltd

Word search

Find the 17 legal terms and expressions hidden in the letters below; 8 read across and 9 read down.

One word has been found for you as an example. The clues listed beneath should help you to find all the words.

U	N	A	N	I	M	O	U	S	A	J	I
N	W	G	V	N	S	M	X	T	D	B	N
J	U	R	I	S	D	I	C	T	I	O	N
U	P	E	B	P	B	S	O	F	S	L	O
S	Q	E	O	E	N	S	K	R	C	J	C
T	I	M	A	C	U	I	R	X	L	I	E
H	G	E	M	T	G	O	F	C	A	Q	N
P	Z	N	U	I	N	N	H	L	I	G	C
L	O	T	D	O	T	A	L	Y	M	I	E
E	N	M	V	N	D	Z	I	E	E	W	F
A	C	T	K	E	C	Y	F	O	R	G	E
S	O	D	S	Q	U	A	T	P	A	E	C

1. To occupy premises belonging to another person unlawfully and without title.
2. Contrary to law or not just.
3. Where everyone votes in the same way.
4. Abbreviation for company.
5. Document setting out the contractual terms agreed between two parties.
6. To copy money or a signature illegally.
7. Legal power over someone or something.
8. Informal word meaning to steal.
9. Close examination of something, especially the examination of the site of a crime by the judge and jury
10. Statute which has been approved by a law-making body
11. Statement which is not true
12. Gray's ______
13. Failure to do something
14. In criminal law, statement made by a person accused in court in answer to the charge
15. Group of shares which are sold
16. Being innocent
17. Legal refusal to accept responsibility or to accept a right

Based on the **Dictionary of Law**, second edition
ISBN 0-948549-33-5
Peter Collin Publishing Ltd

Legal crossword 1

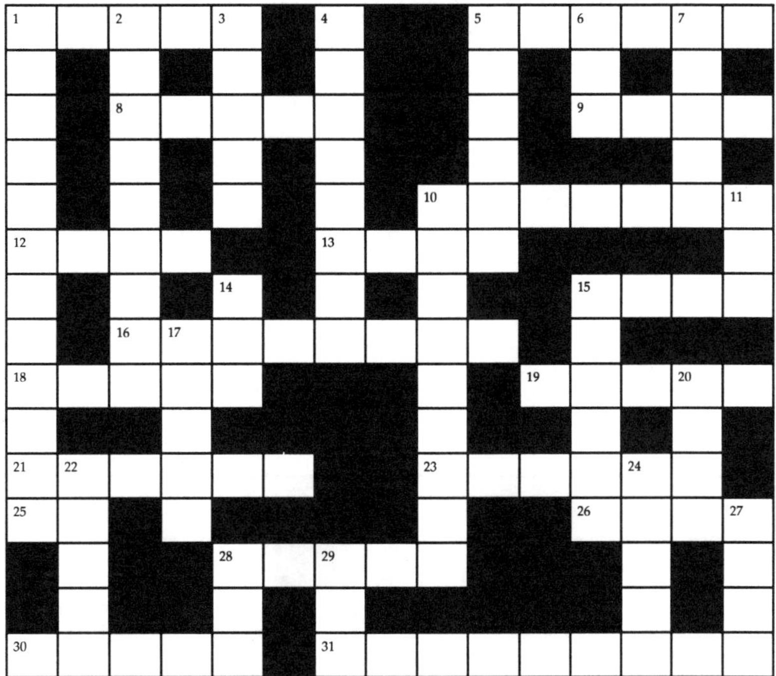

Across

1. To mention or write about something -"We ______ to your letter of May 26th" (5)
5. To take something which is being offered - to say yes (6)
8. The place where a trial is held (5)
9. Civil wrong done to someone and entitling them to claim damages (4)
10. Separate into sections - "The two companies ______ the market between them" (7)
12. One hour, two weeks, half past two... (4)
13. To encourage someone to commit a crime - "To aid and ______" (4)
15. Twelve people who must decide (4)
16. People who receive a legacy from someone who has died
18. Prefix found in words frequently used in legal documents - ______ after/by/for/from/in..(5)
19. Older than eighteen (5)
21. To be against something - "The police have decided to ______ your application for bail." (6)
23. Decide the value - "We must ______ the building for the purposes of insurance." (7)
25. Opposite of yes (2)
26. John married my mother after her divorce: he's my ____-father" (4)
28. Before second (5)
30. Independent nation - say clearly (5)
31. Innocent (3,6)

Down

1. Placing on an official list - "_____ of a trademark" (12)
2. An exact copy of a document - possibly electronically transmitted (9)
3. Unfair, inexact, approximate: "This is a case of _____ justice." (5)
4. A person who brings a lawsuit against another (8)
5. Opposite of convict: "the jury decided to ______ the defendant because there was insufficient evidence" (6)
6. To reduce suddenly - "We are going to ___ all our prices by 25%" (3)
7. Latin expression meaning "by itself" (3,2)
10. The person accused of the crime - the person who is sued (9)
11. Twenty-four hours (3)
14. The number of years a person has been alive (3)
15. Decides (5)
17. Mistake (5)
20. Not to win (4)
22. "That's an interesting ____, but I don't agree with your argument." (5)
24. To take something which is not yours (5)
27. To ask - very formally (4)
28. Money paid for a service (3)
29. To manage - "After my father dies I'll _____ the company" (3)

Based on the **Dictionary of Law**, second edition
ISBN 0-948549-33-5
Peter Collin Publishing Ltd

Communicative crossword 2 sheet A

This crossword is not complete: you have only half the words. The other half are on sheet B. Check that you know the words in your crossword. Then work with a partner who has sheet B to complete the two crosswords. Follow these three rules:

1. Speak only in English

1. Don't say the word in the crossword

1. Don't show your crossword to your partner.

"What's one across?"

→ across, ↓ down

1 S	T	2 A	N	3 D	A	4 R	D	■	5	6		7		8 R
H	■	I	■	E	■	E	■	9	■		■		■	E
A	■	10 D		F		N			■		■		■	P
R	■	■	■	A	■	T	■	11						R
E	■	12 H	■	M	■	■	■		■		■	■	■	I
13 S	C	O	P	E	■	14	■		■	■	15 S	A	N	E
■	■	L	■	■	16					■	U	■	■	V
17 S	H	O	P	■	■		■		■	18 A	B	A	T	E
E	■	G	■	19			20	■	21	■	S	■	■	■
N	■	R	■		■	■	22 C	R	I	M	I	N	A	23 L
24 T		A			25 S	■		■		■	D	■	■	
E	■	P	■	■	26 C					■	I	■	■	
N	■	27 H	28 E	A	R	■		■	29		A			
C	■	■	Y	■	I	■		■		■	R	■	■	
E	■	30 K	E	E	P	■	31			■	32 Y			

Based on the **Dictionary of Law**, second edition
ISBN 0-948549-33-5
Peter Collin Publishing Ltd

Communicative crossword 2 sheet B

This crossword is not complete: you have only half the words. The other half are on sheet A. Check that you know the words in your crossword. Then work with a partner who has sheet A to complete the two crosswords. Follow these three rules:

1. Speak only in English
1. Don't say the word in the crossword
1. Don't show your crossword to your partner.

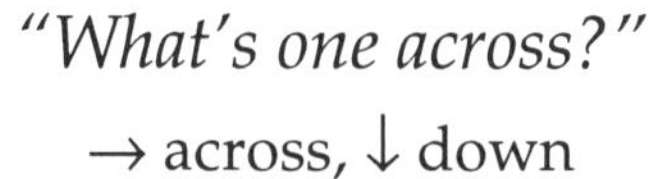

"What's one across?"

→ across, ↓ down

ISBN 0-948549-33-5
Peter Collin Publishing Ltd

Anagrams 2

Read the definitions and put the letters in order to make 15 words connected with the law. Write the words in the grid to find the mystery phrase. The first one has been done for you: *innocent* is the opposite of guilty.

1. Opposite of guilty .... NCEINNOT
2. Maker of illegal fires .... AINORSST
3. A company - the commercial spirit .... EEEINPRRST
4. Save from danger .... CEERSU
5. A country and the people living in it .... AINONT
6. Suggest that something should be done .... CDEEMMNOR
7. A person who is supported financially by someone else .... ADDEENNPT
8. Having a legal duty to do something .... ABDEGILOT
9. Not able to pay debts .... EILNNOSTV
10. An official occasion .... CEEMNORY
11. Kept out, not included .... CDDEELUX
12. Income, money earned, especially from taxation .... EEENRUV
13. To go to law .... AEGIILTT
14. Concerning money .... AACFIILNN
15. A type of lawyer .... CIILOORST

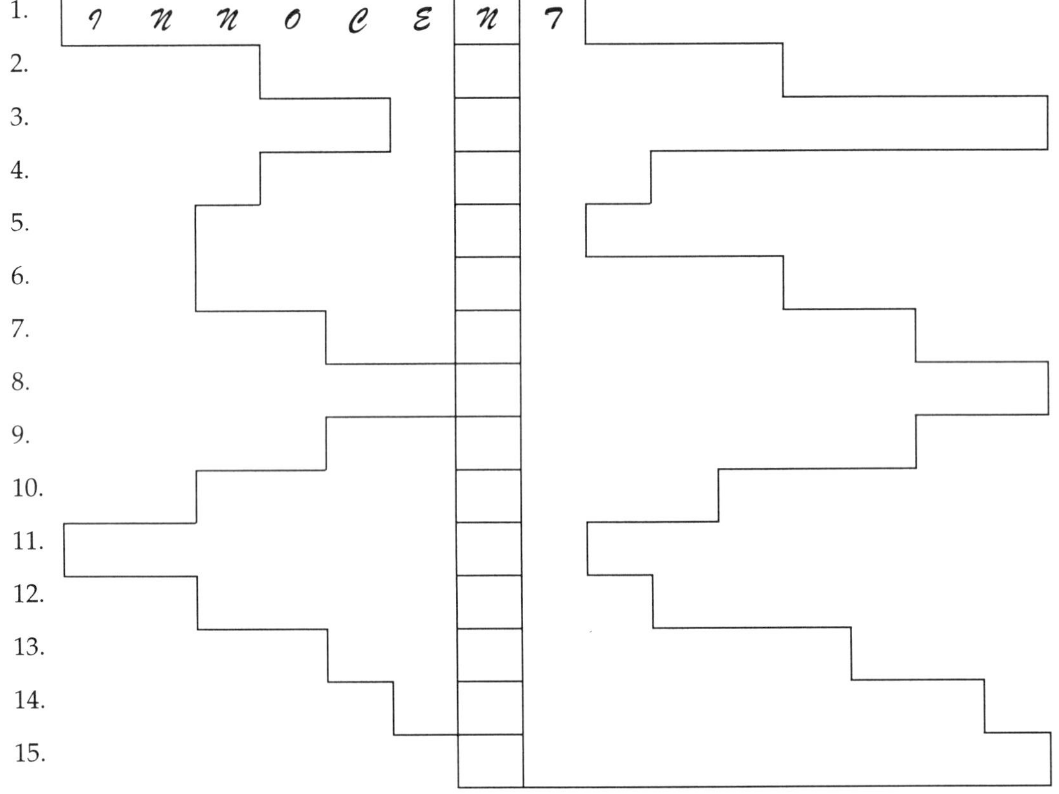

Mystery phrase: crazy — but in Latin

Based on the **Dictionary of Law**, second edition
ISBN 0-948549-33-5
Peter Collin Publishing Ltd

Missing words

Listed below is a selection of terms and expressions associated with the law. Each one has text missing; fill the gap with the correct word from the box on the right of the page. The first has been done for you as an example.

1. Gentleman Usher of the Black _Rod_
2. writ of ________
3. ________ Bailey
4. Queen's ________ Division
5. County ________ Rules
6. ________ of Session
7. yellow ________ contract
8. white ________ crime
9. compulsory purchase ________
10. Lincoln's ________
11. burden of ________
12. Private Member's ________
13. Lord ________ Justice
14. Metropolitan ________ Commissioner
15. Western ________
16. ________ Bureau of Investigation
17. ________ Committee of the House of Lords
18. ________ on recognizance

Bench
Bill
Chief
Circuit
Collar
Court
Court
dog
Federal
Inn
Judicial
Old
order
Police
proof
release
~~Rod~~
summons

ISBN 0-948549-33-5
Peter Collin Publishing Ltd

Communicative crossword 3 sheet A

This crossword is not complete: you have only half the words. The other half are on sheet B. Check that you know the words in your crossword. Then work with a partner who has sheet B to complete the two crosswords. Follow these three rules:

1. Speak only in English.

1. Don't say the word in the crossword.

1. Don't show your crossword to your partner.

> *"What's one across?"*
> → across, ↓ down

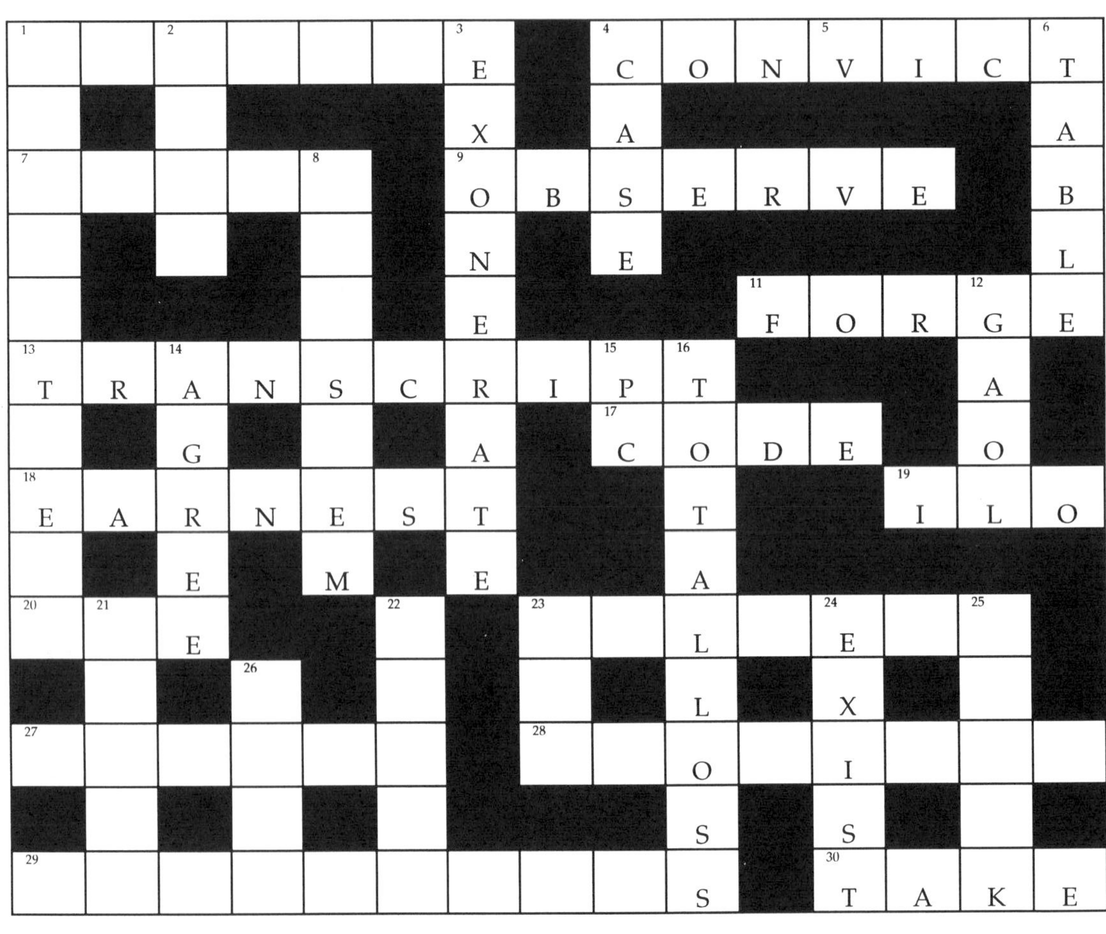

Based on the **Dictionary of Law**, second edition
ISBN 0-948549-33-5
Peter Collin Publishing Ltd

Communicative crossword 3 sheet B

Puzzles & Quizzes

This crossword is not complete: you have only half the words. The other half are on sheet A. Check that you know the words in your crossword. Then work with a partner who has sheet A to complete the two crosswords. Follow these three rules:

1. Speak only in English.

1. Don't say the word in the crossword.

1. Don't show your crossword to your partner.

"What's one across?"

→ across, ↓ down

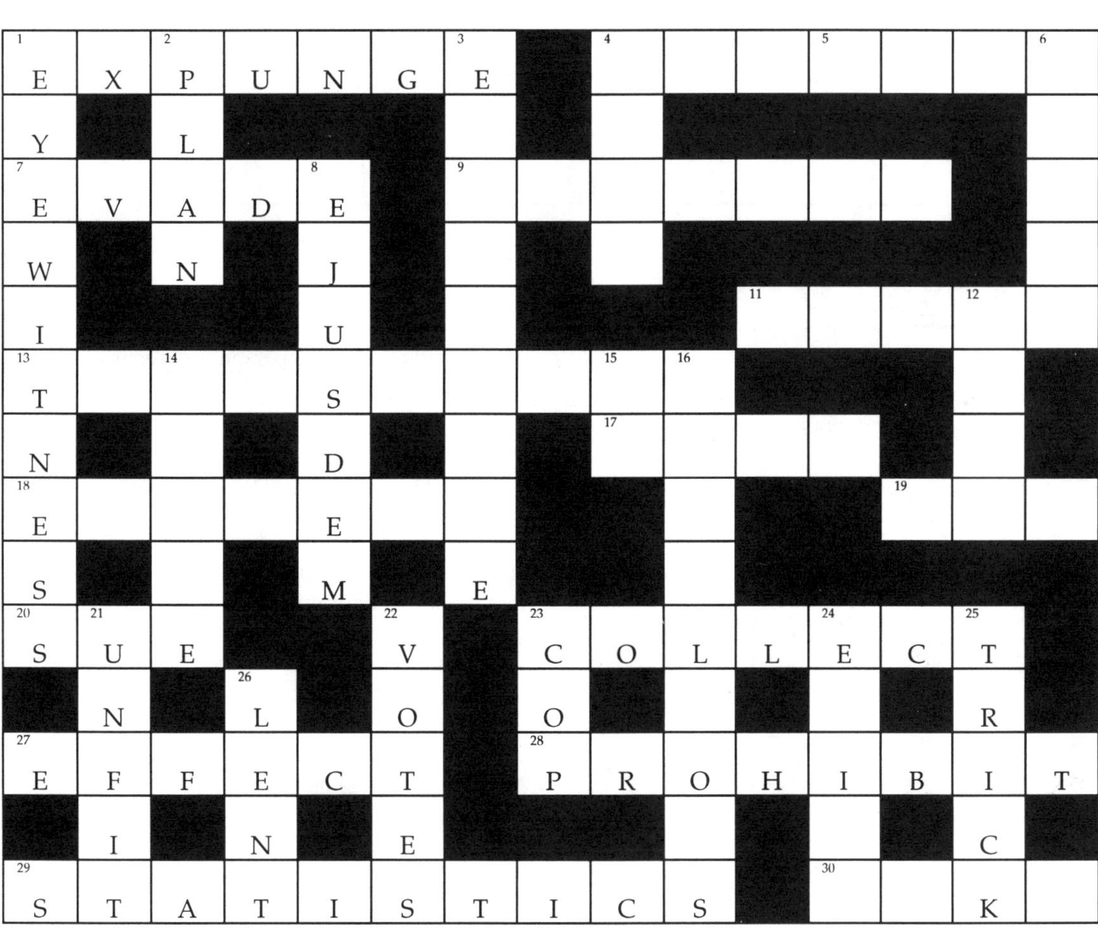

ISBN 0-948549-33-5
Peter Collin Publishing Ltd

Legal crossword 2

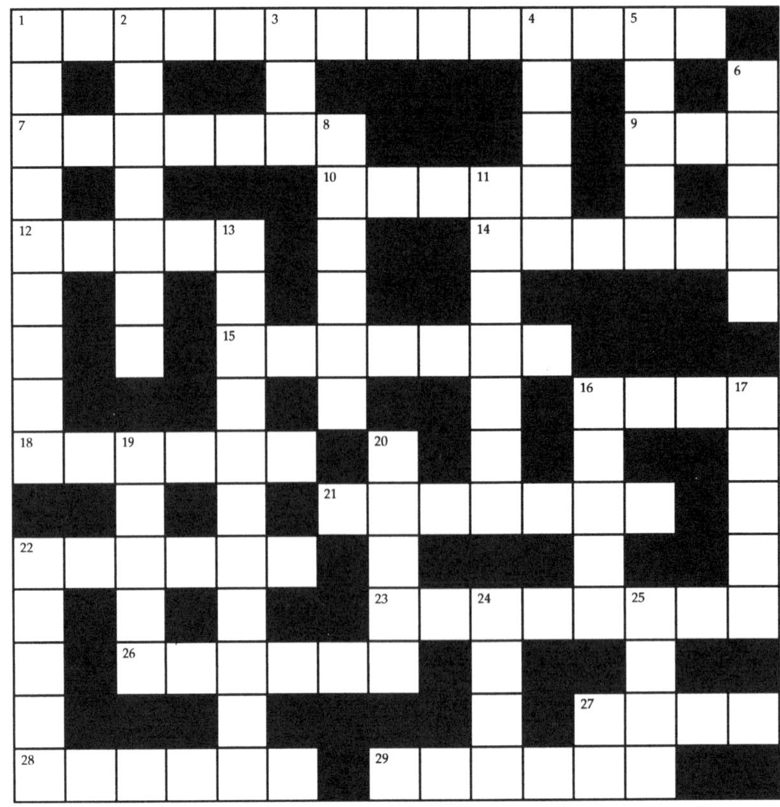

Across

1. Secret (bad?) reason for doing something (8,6)
7. Smallest possible quantity (7)
9. The rules by which a country is governed (3)
10. To try not to do something, e.g. pay taxes (5)
12. To grant that a contract, for example, continues for a further period of time (5)
14. Somebody you borrow from (6)
15. To follow, to inherit (7)
16. Piece, section (4)
18. To slander, to libel (6)
21. Buying and selling shares (7)
22. Not coastal - the interior of a country (6)
23. Not a soldier
26. A thing which has a legal existence (5)
27. Legal document which has been signed, sealed and delivered by the person making it (4)
28. Change which make something better, e.g.: "The group demanded the _____ of the prison system." (6)
29. To pay back all the principal and interest on a loan, to sell a bond for cash (6)

Down

1. Single
2. Agreement by which a person can occupy a property (7)
3. Paper which says you must pay money to someone - informal (3)
4. The business of buying and selling (5)
5. Acceptable, can be used lawfully (5)
6. Decision which settles a dispute, to decide the amount of money to be given to someone (5)
8. Intentionally committing an act from wrong motives (6)
11. Unlawful (7)
13. Where the British parliament meets (11)
16. Relating to punishment (5)
17. To teach someone how to do something (5)
19. Not true, not genuine (5)
20. Forgiveness (5)
22. To make yourself liable to something, e.g.: "You will _____ heavy legal costs if you go to court." (5)
24. Opposite of 5 down, not having legal effect (4)
25. Thing for sale (4)
27. ___ facto or ___ jure (2)

Based on the **Dictionary of Law**, second edition
ISBN 0-948549-33-5
Peter Collin Publishing Ltd

Quiz

How many of these questions can you answer?

1. Which of the following can serve on a British jury:

(yes/no) barristers
(yes/no) judges
(yes/no) solicitors
(yes/no) priests
(yes/no) doctors
(yes/no) Members of Parliament
(yes/no) people who are insane?

2. You ask Mr Smith's job and he tells you he is an *attorney*. Is he American or British?

3. What colour is the card which permits you to live in the USA as a citizen?

4. What is a "white collar criminal"?

5. Who lives at Number Ten?

6. What does 'limited' mean in the name of a company?

7. How many times can a British MP make a maiden speech?

8. What right does the Fifth Amendment guarantee?

9. What is the name given to the personal office of the President of the USA?

10. What colour is used to describe the market where you can buy illicit goods?

11. How many states are there in the USA?

12. If the US Congress is equivalent to the British Commons, what is the British equivalent to the Senate?

13. What is the name of the document which tells people how to dispose of your estate after your death?

14. What is the difference between soft and hard currencies?

15. The United Kingdom is composed of three nations and a province. What are they?

Extension. Work with a partner and write a quiz. Try it on other students.

ISBN 0-948549-33-5
Peter Collin Publishing Ltd

Communicative crossword 4 sheet A

This crossword is not complete: you have only half the words. The other half are on sheet B. Check that you know the words in your crossword. Then work with a partner who has sheet B to complete the two crosswords. Follow these three rules:

1. Speak only in English.
2. Don't say the word in the crossword.
3. Don't show your crossword to your partner.

"What's one across?"

→ across, ↓ down

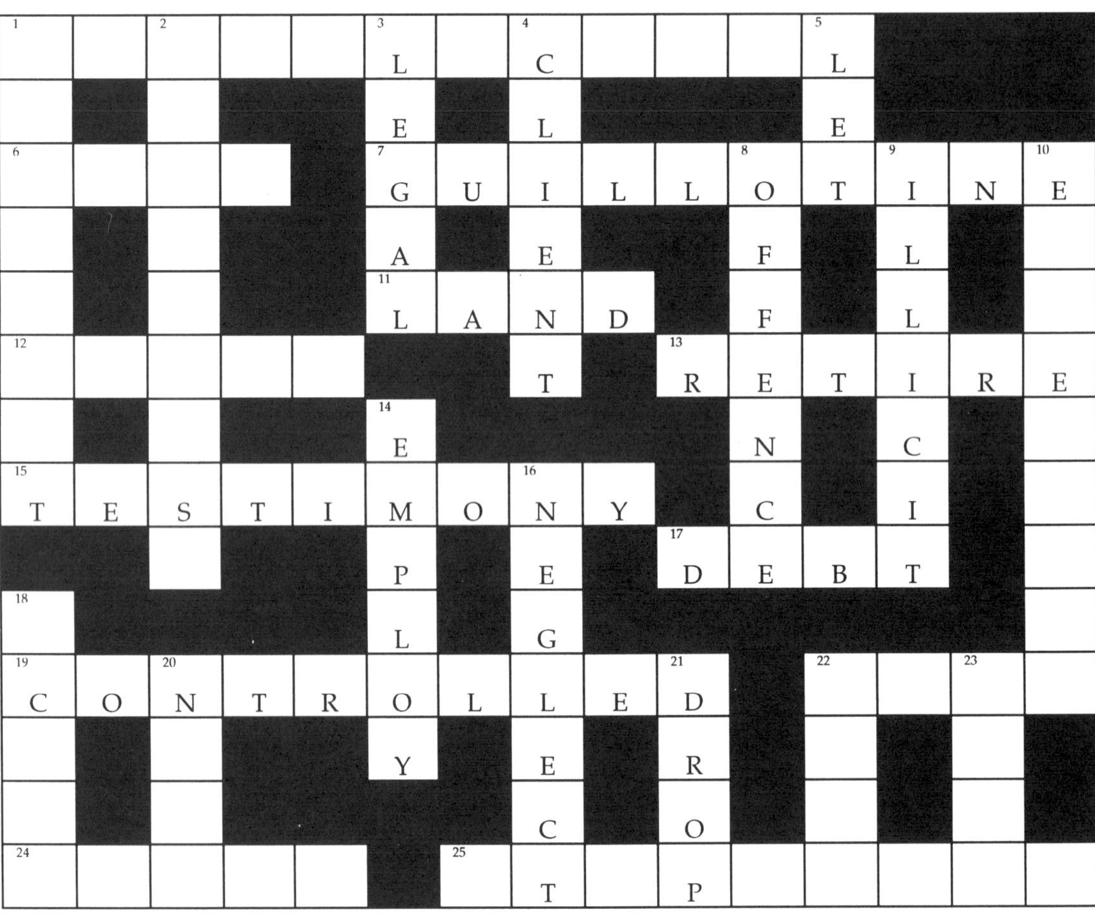

Based on the **Dictionary of Law**, second edition
ISBN 0-948549-33-5
Peter Collin Publishing Ltd

Communicative crossword 4 sheet B

This crossword is not complete: you have only half the words. The other half are on sheet A. Check that you know the words in your crossword. Then work with a partner who has sheet A to complete the two crosswords. Follow these three rules:

1. Speak only in English.
2. Don't say the word in the crossword.
3. Don't show your crossword to your partner.

"What's one across?"

→ across, ↓ down

Based on the **Dictionary of Law**, second edition
ISBN 0-948549-33-5
Peter Collin Publishing Ltd

Peter Collin Publishing

Vocabulary Record Sheet

WORD	CLASS	NOTES *Translation or definition, example...*

Based on the **Dictionary of Law**, second edition
ISBN 0-948549-33-5
Peter Collin Publishing Ltd

Answer key

Word building

Word association 1: missing links *(p.1)*

1.law 2. court 3. jury 4. contract 5. claim

Word formation: nouns *(p.2)*

1. The offer of a large amount of money was his **inducement** to steal the plans.
2. There will be an **enforcement** of the terms of the contract.
3. He has **authorization** to act on our behalf.
4. The **rescission** of the contract occurred last year.
5. You face **punishment** for hitting the policeman.
6. His **prosecution** for embezzlement was reported in the newspaper.
7. The **investigation** covered irregularities in share dealings.
8. His **inheritance** from his grandfather was £10,0000.
9. The witness' **cancellation** of today's appointment took place last week.
10. They got into an **argument** with the judge over the relevance of the documents to the case.

Latin pair-up *(p.3)*

1. *bona fide* 2. *inter alia* 3. *caveat emptor* 4. *obiter dicta* 5. *vice versa* 6. *viva voce* 7. *compos mentis* 8. *sui generis* 9. *toties quoties* 10. *inter vivos* 11. *habeas corpus* 12. *ipso facto* 13. *doli capax* 14. *per capita* 15. *prima facie*

Plural formation *(p.4)*

1. referenda 2. preservation orders 3. bureaux 4. criteria 5. policewomen 6. misdemeanours 7. corpora 8. notaries public 9. memoranda 10. jurymen 11. rejoinders 12. moratoria 13. appendices 14. injunctions 15. provisions 16. corrigenda 17. presidents-elect 18. LJJ 19. quangos 20. dicta

Word formation: adjectives *(p.5)*

1. insolvent 2. insane 3. guilty 4. incompetent 5. responsible 6. intoxicated 7. fit 8. exempt 9. legal 10. legitimate

Word association 2: partnerships *(p.6)*

Exercise 1.

1. break a law 2. commit a crime 3. cross examine a witness 4. charge a fee 5. declare an interest 6. enter a market 7. evade taxes 8. hear a case 9. negotiate terms 10. return a verdict

Exercise 2.

1. breaking the law 2. negotiate terms 3. returned a verdict 4. enter the market 5. evade taxes 6. heard the case 7. cross examining the witness 8. commit the crime 9. declare an interest 10. charge a fee

Opposites 1: prefixes *(p.7)*

Exercise 1.

-il

1. illegal 2. illegitimate

-im

1. immoral 2. immovable 3. imperfect 4. improper

-in

1. inadmissible 2. incapable 3. incompetent 4. incorrect 5. independent 6. insane 7. insolvent 8. invalid

-ir

1. irreconcilable 2. irrecoverable 3. irregular 4. irrelevant

-un

1. unconfirmed 2. uninsured 3. unjust 4. unlawful 5. unprofessional 6. unreliable

Exercise 2.

1. inadmissible 2. incorrect 3. unreliable 4. improper 5. imperfect 6. irrelevant 7. unconfirmed 8. illegal 9. insolvent 10. invalid 11. irrecoverable 12. independent

Word formation: verbs *(p.8)*

Exercise 1.

1. to abrogate 2. to abstain 3. to adjourn 4. to brief 5. to confine 6. to corroborate 7. to cross-examine 8. to decide 9. to declare 10. to defer to discriminate 12. to embezzle 13. to exclude 14. to immigrate 15. to incite 16. to justify 17. to misappropriate 18. to poll 19. to prosecute 20. to provoke 21. to represent 22. to terminate 23. to veto 24. to violate

Word association 3: mind maps *(p.9)*

Exercise 1.

1. stolen 2. burglar 3. to pick (someone's) pocket 4. to mug 5. housebreaking 6. shoplifter 7. kleptomania 8. thief 9. to hold up (a place) 10. stolen property

Parts of speech

Nouns: name the crime 1 *(p.10)*

1. assault 2. treason 3. piracy 4. burglary 5. blackmail 6. extortion 7. fraud 8. bigamy 9. assassination 10. murder 11. manslaughter 12. forgery 13. bribery 14. slander 15. arson 16. robbery 17. theft 18. mugging 19. perjury 20. espionage 21. embezzlement 22. libel

Nouns: politics *(p.11)*

1. constitution. 2. spokesman 3. poll 4. membership 5. devolution 6. legislation 7. Houses 8. recess 9. leak 10. policy 11. leader 12. abstentions 13. veto 14. consensus 15. budget

Nouns: name the crime 2 *(p.12)*

1. burglary 2. murder 3. embezzlement or fraud 4. piracy 5. smuggling 6. bigamy 7. bribery 8. espionage 9. forgery 10. blackmail

Adjectives 1 *(p.13)*

1. preliminary 2. exemplary 3. liable 4. joint 5. out-of-court 6. concurrent 7. flagrant 8. bankrupt 9. overdue 10. civil 11. exempt 12. hostile 13. intentional 14. consecutive 15. germane

Adjectives 2 *(p.14)*

1. guilty 2. dual 3. heavy 4. ostensible 5. competent 6. legal 7. conditional 8. unlimited 9. wilful 10. domestic 11. biased 12. reciprocal 13. official 14. final 15. equal

Verbs *(p.15)*

1. reach 2. evict 3. approve 4. withhold 5. earn 6. bribe 7. rescind 8. adjourn 9. employ 10. testify 11. issue 12. obligate 13. dismiss 14. recommend 15. arbitrate

Verbs: past tense ~ regular verbs *(p.16)*

1. confessed 2. granted 3. accused 4. imprisoned 5. engaged 6. pleaded 7. charged. 8. arrested 9. released 10. fined. 11. dropped 12. seized 13. served 14. awarded 15. acquitted

Verbs: mixed tenses 1 *(p.17)*

1. disclaimed 2. offering 3. appeal 4. embezzling 5. manipulating 6. value 7. advised 8. legislated 9. disclose. 10. established 11. followed 12. imposed 13. committed 14. prevent 15. preclude

Verbs: mixed tenses 2 *(p.18)*

1. refrain 2. overturn 3. corroborate 4. sentenced 5. sued 6. convicted 7. forfeit 8. found 9. infringes 10. recovered 11. blackmailing 12. promised 13. prohibits 14. arranged 15. exonerated

Phrasal verbs 1 *(p.19)*

1.	g	9.	n
2.	e	10.	o
3.	p	11.	d
4.	b	12.	h
5.	i	13.	c
6.	l	14.	f
7.	k	15.	a
8.	m	16.	j

Phrasal verbs 2 *(p.20)*

1. broken up 2. passed off 3. took ... in 4. breaking into 5. wound up 6. bring ... forward 7. takes over 8. broke off 9. held up 10. taken over 11. broke down 12. wound up 13. held up 14. holding up 15. handed down 16. put ... into 17. brought up 18. put ... down 19. brought in 20. call in

Verbs: active/passive *(p.21)*

1. The driver of the stolen car was arrested by the constable.
2. The witness was asked by the judge to write the name on a piece of paper.
3. A writ is going to be issued by the company to prevent the trade union from going on strike.
4. His will was written in 1990.
5. The damage is itemized in the pleading.
6. I was left £5,000 by my grandmother in her will.
7. The company was granted a two-week stay of execution by the court.
8. Detectives should be called in to help in the murder hunt.
9. Judicial review is being sought by the applicant to quash the order.
10. The wounded man was left lying on the road.

Adverbs *(p.22)*

Here

1.	hereafter	in the future - from the production of this document on
2.	hereby	resulting from this document
3.	herein	appearing somewhere in this document
4.	hereinafter	listed later in this document
5.	hereof	relating to this document or part of it
6.	hereto	following this document
7.	heretofore	previous to the production of this document
8.	herunder	mentioned in this same section of this document
9.	herewith	accompanying this document

There

1.	thereafter	from the production of that document until now
2.	thereby	resulting from that document or decision
3.	therefore	for that reason or purpose
4.	therein	appearing somewhere in that document
5.	thereinafter	listed later in that document
6.	thereinbefore	mentioned previously in that document
7.	thereinunder	mentioned in that section of that document
8.	thereof	relating to that document
9.	thereto	following that document
10.	theretofore	in the time before that document was produced
11.	therewith	accompanying that document

Prepositions *(p.23)*

1. It says in the newspaper that he's been evading ~~of~~ income tax.
2. The prosecution tried to discredit ~~at~~ the defence witness.
3. I am writing in∧ behalf of Mr and Mrs Smith... ***on***
4. I would like to report ~~of~~ a theft.
5. He was awarded £100,000 to compensate ~~of~~∧ the damages caused by the manufacturer. ***for***
6. The directors of the firm were accused∧ insider trading. ***of***
7. If you don't tell me you'll be charged ~~to~~∧ withholding evidence. ***with***
8. In view of your failure to pay, I have instructed ~~to~~ my solicitors to start proceedings immediately.
9. We have referred your question ~~at~~∧ the tribunal and hope to have an answer for you in the next few days. ***to***
10. After six months in prison she will be eligible ~~to~~∧ parole. ***for***
11. The next national holiday falls ~~in~~∧ a Monday. ***on***
12. They decided to sue ~~at~~ the landlord for failure to maintain the property.
13. During the appeal he claimed that the original judge had been biased in favour ~~to~~∧ the plaintiff. ***of***
14. The defendant was negligent ~~to~~∧ carrying out his duties as a trustee. ***in***
15. The company was declared to be ~~of~~∧ a state of insolvency. ***in***
16. My client disagrees with clause 6 of the contract which expressly forbids ~~to~~ sales in the USA.

17. The judge ruled that her evidence was inadmissible and it was expunged∧ the report. *from*
18. Does the bill include ~~of~~ VAT or is that extra?
19. The judge acquitted ~~to~~ the husband but imposed a £250 fine on the wife.
20. He was found guilty of all charges and sentenced∧ five years in prison. *to*

Pronunciation

Word stress *(p.24)*

GROUP 1 ❶②③ 1. evidence 2. innocent 3. companies 4. prosecute 5. government 6. minister 7. treasury

GROUP 2 ①❷③ 1. acquittal 2. forensic 3. decision 4. indictment 5. opinion 6. performance 7. example 8. selection 9. consider 10. embezzled 11. director 12. department 13. corruption. 14. insider

GROUP 3 ①②❸
1. disapproved 2. incorrect 3. recommend 4. employees

Verbs & nouns *(p.25)*

	n/vb	❶②	①❷
1.	verb		×
2.	noun	×	
3.	noun	×	
4.	verb		×
5.	noun	×	
6.	verb		×
7.	verb		×
8.	noun	×	
9.	noun	×	
10.	verb		×
11.	verb		×
12.	noun	×	
13.	noun	×	
14.	verb		×
15.	noun	×	
16.	verb		×
17.	verb		×
18.	noun	×	
19.	verb		×
20.	noun	×	

Present simple *(p.26)*

	1 /s/	2 /z/	3 /Iz/
1. pleads		×	
2. helps	×		
3. dismisses			×
4. commutes	×		
5. collects	×		
6. claims		×	
7. discharges			×
8. leases			×
9. repudiates	×		
10. summarises			×
11. disqualifies		×	
12. acquits	×		
13. corroborates	×		
14. intends		×	
15. recommends		×	
16. owns		×	
17. discriminates	×		
18. employs		×	
19. assesses			×
20. taxes			×
21. signs		×	
22. falls		×	
23. corrupts	×		
24. controls		×	
25. advises			×

Past tense & past participle *(p.27)*

	1 /t/	2 /d/	3 /Id/
1. disciplined		×	
2. discriminated			×
3. presumed		×	
4. recovered		×	
5. reformed		×	
6. despatched	×		
7. surrendered		×	
8. blackmailed		×	
9. blacklisted			×
10. promised	×		
11. swindled		×	
12. practised	×		
13. represented			×
14. recorded			×
15. adjourned		×	
16. caused		×	
17. sentenced	×		
18. pardoned		×	
19. traded			×
20. summoned		×	
21. financed	×		
22. based	×		
23. published	×		
24. empowered		×	
25. decided			×

Vocabulary in context

Multiple meanings *(p.28)*

1. convention 2. principal 3. article 4. estate 5. due 6. state 7. interest 8. express

Test your criminal slang *(p.29)*

1. a fence 2. a brief 3. a mug 4. a screw 5. a scam 6. a nark 7. bent 8. inside 9. hot 10. the law 11. to nick 12. to blag 13. to grass 14. to launder money

Categories *(p.30)*

Crimes against the person:

murder — manslaughter
abduction — assault
grievous bodily harm — battery
blackmail

Crimes against property:

burglary — theft
criminal damage — robbery
forgery

Sexual offences:

rape — criminal damage
buggery — bigamy

Categories *(p.30) contd.*

Political offences:	
treason	sedition
Offences against justice:	
perjury	perverting the course of justice
Public order offences:	
obscenity	breach of the peace
Road traffic offences:	
reckless driving	

Odd one out *(p.31)*

1. alone: the others are marital states
2. judge: the others are types of lawyer
3. arson: the others are types of theft
4. convict: the others happen at the beginning of the legal process
5. right: the others are things you have to do
6. blackmail: the others are types of unlawful killing
7. herewith: the others refer to something in the same document as they appear in
8. plea: the others are ways to guarantee money borrowed
9. condemnation: the others refer to leniency
10. execution: the others are methods
11. discredit: the others are words about giving
12. ransom: the others refer to taking and holding a person unlawfully
13. accidentally: the others describe intentional actions
14. appeal: it can only happen after one of the others
15. royalty: the others do not refer to payment, only to rights
16. contract: the others are relationships
17. witness: the others refer to the person who charged with a crime
18. deny: it can be the opposite of any of the others

Opposites 2 *(p.32)*

Exercise 1.

accidental ~ deliberate
acquit ~ convict
borrow ~ lend
bring forward ~ defer
cancel ~ confirm
civil ~ criminal
confess ~ deny
defence ~ prosecution
defendant ~ plaintiff
guilty ~ innocent
imprison ~ release
landlord ~ tenant

Exercise 2.

1. guilty 2. convict 3. defer 4. defendant
5. tenant 6. confess 7. borrow 8. civil 9. release
10. defence 11. cancel 12. deliberate

Abbreviations *(p.33)*

1. also known as 2. any other business 3. cash on delivery 4. District Attorney 5. errors and omissions excepted 6. for example (from Latin *exempli gratia*) 7. free on board 8. Federal Bureau of Investigation 9. Foreign Office 10. grievous bodily harm 11. gross national product 12. identity 13. incorporated 14. I owe you 15. Justice of the Peace 16. letter of credit 17. Member of the European Parliament 18. used to show that a letter has been signed on behalf of someone else (from Latin *per procurationem*) 19. Public Limited Company 20. proportional representation 21. Queen's Counsel 22. received 23. versus 24. value added tax

Who's speaking? *(p.34)*

1. prosecution counsel
2. Mark Barry, witness
3. a policeman, witness
4. a passer by, witness
5. Mr Swan, defendant
6. Ellen Barry, witness
7. Mr Swan's secretary, witness
8. judge
9. foreman of the jury
10. defence counsel

Mr Swan had previously lent money to Mr Barry who had made no attempt to pay him back. Mr Swan took the day's takings from his business (about £1,000) and told his secretary that he was going to the bank. In fact he intended to find Mr Barry and frighten him into returning the money. He took a pistol, which he loaded so as to be able to defend himself if something went wrong. Mr Swan found Mr Barry in the street and demanded his money. They began to argue and Mr Swan produced the gun. Mr Barry tried to run away. In the heat of the moment Mr Swan lost his temper and shot Mr Barry in the leg. He walked away but was arrested within a few minutes. He was charged with assault and malicious wounding and found guilty. He was sentenced to eight years in prison.

The courts *(p.35)*

1.	h	10.	p
2.	i	11.	r
3.	g	12.	o
4.	j	13.	d
5.	k	14.	a
6.	l	15.	m
7.	b	16.	c
8.	n	17.	e
9.	q	18.	f

What am I? *(p.36)*

1. h	2. g	3. l
4. i	5. a	6. j
7. k	8. b	9. c
10. d	11. f	12. e

Puzzles & quizzes

Anagrams 1 *(p.37)*

1. A **C** C O M P L I C E
2. P R **O** C E D U R E S
3. P R I **N** C I P A L
4. E Q U I **T** A B L E
5. I N T **E** N T I O N
6. T E **M** P O R A R Y
7. A **P** P O I N T M E N T
8. **T** A X A T I O N
9. M **O** R T G A G E
10. D E **F** E R R E D
11. P R E **C** E D E N T
12. F R I V **O** L O U S
13. O C C **U** P A N C Y
14. C O **R** P O R A T E
15. E **T** I Q U E T T E

Word search *(p.40)*

U	N	A	N	I	M	O	U	S	A	J	I
N	W	G	V	N	S	M	X	T	D	B	N
J	U	R	I	S	D	I	C	T	I	O	N
U	P	E	B	P	B	S	O	F	S	L	O
S	Q	E	O	E	N	S	K	R	C	J	C
T	I	M	A	C	U	I	R	X	L	T	E
H	G	E	M	T	G	O	F	C	A	Q	N
P	Z	N	U	I	N	N	H	L	I	G	C
L	O	T	D	O	T	A	L	Y	M	I	E
E	N	M	V	N	D	Z	I	E	E	W	F
A	C	T	K	E	C	Y	F	O	R	G	E
S	O	D	S	Q	U	A	T	P	A	E	C

Legal crossword 1 *(p.41)*

R	E	F	E	R		L			A	C	C	E	P	T
E		A		O		I			C		U		E	
G		C	O	U	R	T			Q		T	O	R	T
I		S		G		I			U				S	
S		I		H		G		D	I	V	I	D	E	D
T	I	M	E			A	B	E	T					A
R		I		A		N		F			J	U	R	Y
A		L	E	G	A	T	E	E	S		U			
T	H	E	R	E				N		A	D	U	L	T
I			R					D			G		O	
O	P	P	O	S	E			A	S	S	E	S	S	
N	O		R					N			S	T	E	P
	I			F	I	R	S	T				E		R
	N			E		U						A		A
S	T	A	T	E		N	O	T	G	U	I	L	T	Y

Anagrams 2 *(p.44)*

1. INNOCE**N**T
2. ARS**O**NIST
3. E**N**TERPRISE
4. RES**C**UE
5. NATI**O**N
6. RECO**M**MEND
7. DE**P**ENDANT
8. **O**BLIGATED
9. IN**S**OLVENT
10. CERE**M**ONY
11. EXCLUD**E**D
12. REVE**N**UE
13. LI**T**IGATE
14. F**I**NANCIAL
15. **S**OLICITOR

Missing words *(p.45)*

1. Rod
2. summons
3. Old
4. Bench
5. Court
6. Court
7. dog
8. collar
9. order
10. proof
11. Inn
12. Bill
13. Chief
14. Police
15. Circuit
16. Federal
17. Judicial
18. release

Legal crossword 2 *(p.48)*

U	L	T	E	R	I	O	R	M	O	T	I	V	E	
N		E			O					R		A		A
M	I	N	I	M	U	M				A		L	A	W
A		A				A	V	O	I	D		I		A
R	E	N	E	W		L			L	E	N	D	E	R
R		C		E		I			L					D
I		Y		S	U	C	C	E	E	D				
E				T		E			G		P	A	R	T
D	E	F	A	M	E		M		A		E			R
		A		I		D	E	A	L	I	N	G		A
I	N	L	A	N	D		R				A			I
N		S		S			C	I	V	I	L	I	A	N
C		E	N	T	I	T	Y		O			T		
U				E					I		D	E	E	D
R	E	F	O	R	M		R	E	D	E	E	M		

Quiz *(p.49)*

1. none of them
2. American
3. green
4. a business person or office worker who uses their job to steal or commit fraud
5. The British Prime Minister
6. that the amount of money to be paid out in the event of business failure is limited to the original investment
7. once — it is his or her first speech on becoming an MP for the first time
8. the right to remain silent
9. Oval
10. black
11. fifty (plus the District of Columbia)
12. House of Lords
13. will
14. hard currencies can be used and exchanged easily on international markets
15. England, Scotland, Wales & Northern Ireland

Specialist Dictionaries

English Dictionary for Students

A new general English dictionary written for intermediate to upper-intermediate level students. The Dictionary includes up-to-date coverage of English with over 20,000 terms, each clearly defined using a limited vocabulary of just 1500 words. Includes vocabulary used in TOEFL, TOEIC, UCLES, SAT and similar English exams.

- written for learners of English
- covers British and American terms
- phonetic pronunciation
- example sentences and quotations show usage

ISBN 1-901659-06-2 720pages paperback £9.95 / US$15.95

Check your Vocabulary for English

A companion workbook of exercises, puzzles, crosswords and word games to test general English skills. Provides material suitable for students taking Cambridge First Certificate/C.A.E level exams.

ISBN 1-901659-11-9 £5.95 / US$9.95

For full details on our complete range of dictionaries and workbooks, visit our web site: **www.pcp.co.uk** or use the form below to request further information.

English Dictionaries

English Dictionary for Students	1-901659-06-2	❑
Accounting	0-948549-27-0	❑
Agriculture, 2nd ed	0-948549-78-5	❑
American Business	0-948549-11-4	❑
Automobile Engineering	0-948549-66-1	❑
Banking & Finance	0-948549-12-2	❑
Business, 2nd ed	0-948549-51-3	❑
Computing, 3rd ed	1-901659-04-6	❑
Ecology & Environment, 3ed	0-948549-74-2	❑
Government & Politics, 2ed	0-948549-89-0	❑
Hotel, Tourism, Catering Management	0-948549-40-8	❑
Human Resources & Personnel, 2ed	0-948549-79-3	❑
Information Technology, 2nd ed	0-948549-88-2	❑
Law, 2nd ed	0-948549-33-5	❑
Library & Information Management	0-948549-68-8	❑
Marketing, 2nd ed	0-948549-73-4	❑
Medicine, 2nd ed	0-948549-36-X	❑
Printing & Publishing, 2nd ed	0-948549-99-8	❑
Science & Technology	0-948549-67-X	❑

Vocabulary Workbooks

Banking & Finance	0-948549-96-3	❑
Business	0-948549-72-6	❑
Computing	0-948549-58-0	❑
Colloquial English	0-948549-97-1	❑
English	1-901659-11-9	❑
Hotels, Tourism, Catering	0-948549-75-0	❑
Law, 2nd edition	1-901659-21-6	❑
Medicine	0-948549-59-9	❑

Professional/General

Astronomy	0-948549-43-2	❑
Economics	0-948549-91-2	❑
Multimedia, 2nd ed	1-901659-01-1	❑
PC & the Internet, 2nd ed	1-901659-12-7	❑
Bradford Crossword Solver, 3rd ed	1-901659-03-8	❑

Bilingual Dictionaries

French-English/English-French Dictionaries ❑
German-English/English-German Dictionaries ❑
Spanish-English/English-Spanish Dictionaries ❑

Name:..
Address:..
....
....
......................................Postcode:......................Country:......................

Peter Collin Publishing Ltd
1 Cambridge Road
Teddington, TW11 8DT - UK
tel: +44 181 943 3386 fax: +44 181 943 1673 email: info@pcp.co.uk
web site: www.pcp.co.uk